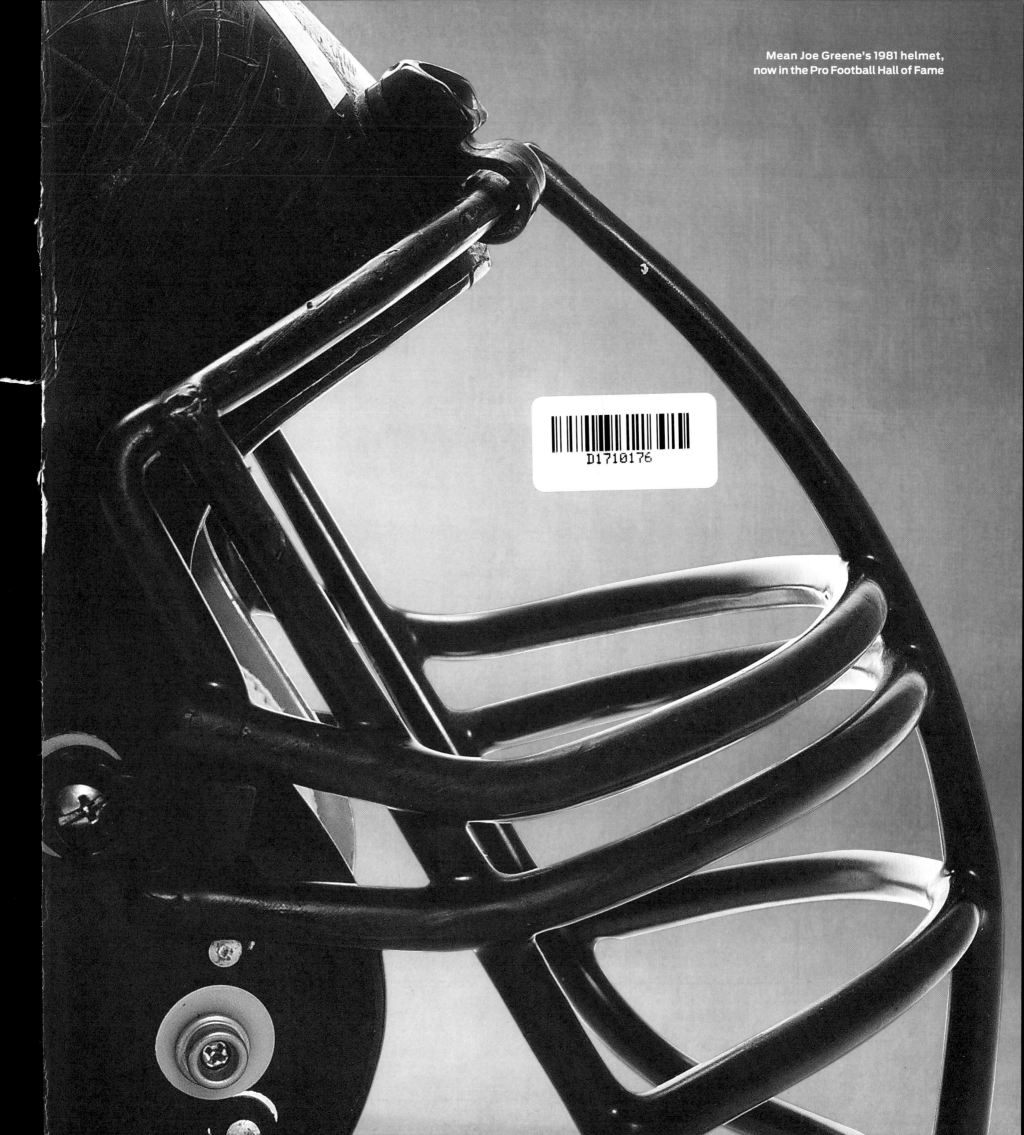

Mean Joe Greene's 1981 helmet,
now in the Pro Football Hall of Fame

D1710176

Sports Illustrated

PITTSBURGH
STEELERS
Pride in Black and Gold

From Super Bowl XLIII, the Steelers' sixth championship ring

Troy Polamalu, equally intelligent and aggressive, has set the tone for the modern Steelers defenses.

Sports Illustrated

PITTSBURGH
STEELERS
Pride in Black and Gold

Heinz Field, aglow for a night game, supplanted Three Rivers as the Steelers' home field in 2001.

> " It was a team that filled a void and captured a city. "

JEROME BETTIS	CASEY HAMPTON	BEN ROETHLISBERGER
ROCKY BLEIER	FRANCO HARRIS	ANDY RUSSELL
MEL BLOUNT	JAMES HARRISON	AARON SMITH
TERRY BRADSHAW	ERNIE HOLMES	JOHN STALLWORTH
JACK BUTLER	JOHN HENRY JOHNSON	ERNIE STAUTNER
DERMONTTI DAWSON	CARNELL LAKE	LYNN SWANN
ALAN FANECA	JACK LAMBERT	HINES WARD
JOE GREENE	BOBBY LAYNE	MIKE WEBSTER
L.C. GREENWOOD	ELBIE NICKEL	DWIGHT WHITE
JACK HAM	TROY POLAMALU	ROD WOODSON

MARK MRAVIC
BILL SYKEN
Editors

HOFFMAN NOLI DESIGN
Art Direction

CRISTINA SCALET
Photo Editor

KEVIN KERR
Copy Editor

JOSH DENKIN
Designer

MATT GAGNE
Reporter

STEFANIE KAUFMAN
Project Manager

The indomitable
Joe Greene is one of 18
Steelers enshrined in
the Hall of Fame.

rd & 14 ▬ Ball on 16 3rd Q

Ohio-born Ben Roethlisberger is in his element
in the Burgh, as evidenced by his 49–15 record
at Heinz in his first eight seasons.

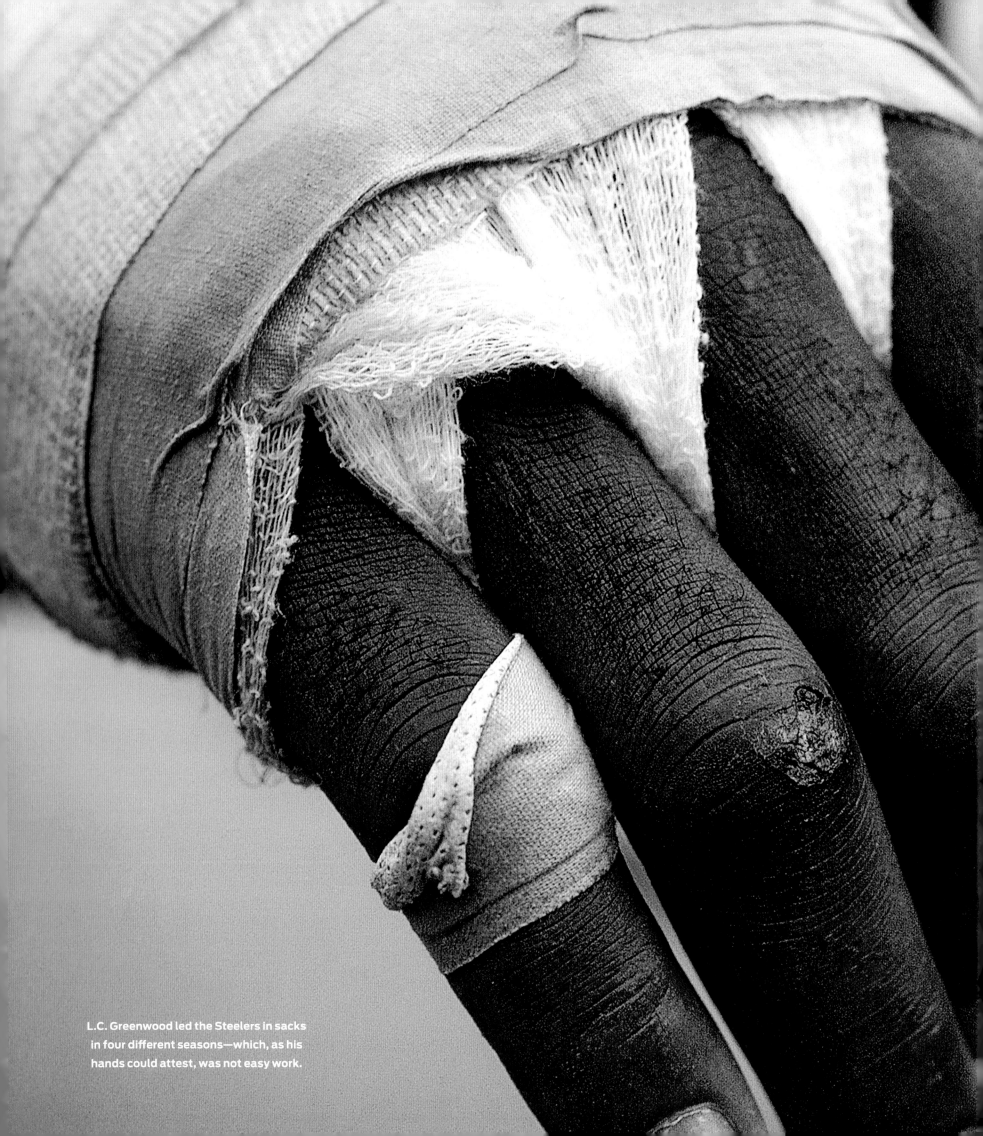

L.C. Greenwood led the Steelers in sacks in four different seasons—which, as his hands could attest, was not easy work.

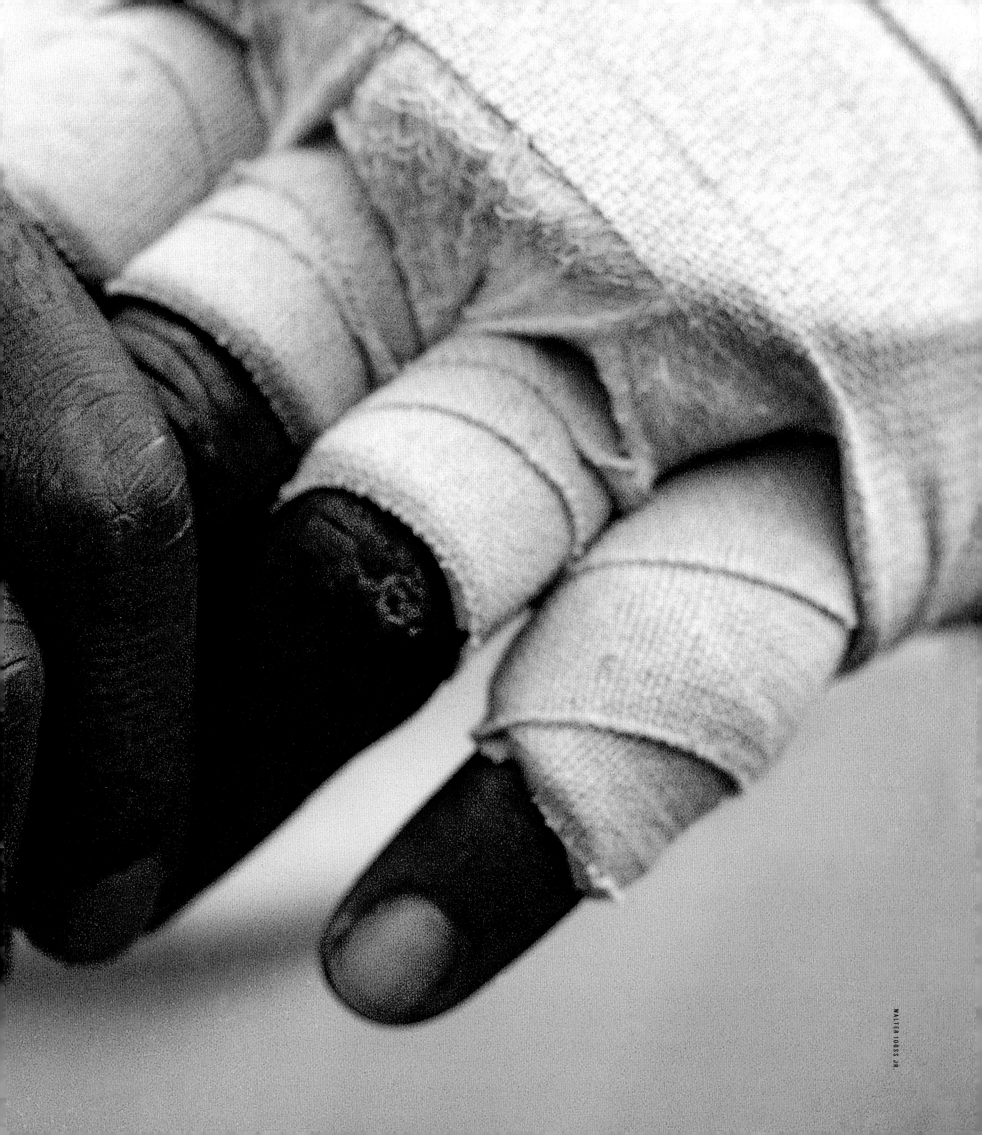

Terry Bradshaw commanded his troops
from his own end zone in a 38–16
victory at Kansas City in 1971.

THE HEART OF THE CITY

Tough, consistent, well-managed, successful—the Steelers are as fine a franchise as there is American sports, a civic symbol and the lifeblood of football-crazed Pittsburgh

BY TIM LAYDEN

THE SCENE WAS UNIQUE AND beyond simple description, yet oddly familiar in this place and in this world. Here was the fourth Sunday in January 2011, and the Pittsburgh Steelers had beaten the New York Jets 24–19 to win the AFC Championship Game and advance to Super Bowl XLV. Night had long since fallen on Heinz Field and the temperature was now into the low teens and still dropping. Yet still the stadium shook in communal celebration, hardly a soul among more than 66,000 having chosen to leave. Veteran cornerback Ike Taylor stood shirtless on a bench, beseeching the crowd to sing the team's kitschy song *(Steelers Goin' to the Super Bowl. . .)*. Behemoth nosetackle Casey Hampton ran slapping the hands of fans who reached over the wall that bordered the grass. Steam rose from the field and from the seats and far beyond, into the parking lots and highways and onto the stony hillsides that form the geologic walls of the city and once provided raw materials for its bedrock industry.

The team has borne the Rooney stamp since its founding by the Chief in '33.

In this moment it might have been any autumn afternoon in the 1950s or '60s, when the Steelers were beaten by some member of NFL royalty—the Giants or the Bears or the Packers—but dished out enough punishment in defeat to make their fans proud. It might have been Dec. 23, 1972, when Franco Harris's Immaculate Reception sealed the first postseason win in Steelers history and sent them to the AFC Championship Game, drilling home a critical rivet in the bridge from incompetence to greatness. It might have been three years later,

The Steelers' fortunes turned on bountiful drafts, including the 1970 pick of Bradshaw that brought smiles to Art and Dan.

when Steelers fans first raised broadcaster Myron Cope's Terrible Towels, swatches of yellow terry cloth that would come to symbolize the franchise. Because these moments are of a kind, measuring the kinship between a city and a team.

There is always a bond connecting any town and its sports teams. Often the bond is built on success and layered a mile wide and an inch thick, fickle supporters always with one foot in and one foot out,

waiting for just the slightest excuse to shred their season ticket orders and junk their replica jerseys. In these towns, and with these teams, support is just a diversion, like watching a hot new television show. Yet there are other places where the line that separates the fan from the franchise is scarcely distinguishable, where love is displayed most openly on game day but never lies dormant.

Pittsburgh is one of these places. The Steelers are one of these teams.

"The Steelers are the best example of what the city's personality is. This is a blue-collar, shot-and-beer town. The fans get up for big games. They're like us. They're good, honest working people who come out to be entertained. They lead a tough life, and they like a team with a tough defense because that's where character shows. We have it. We play tough and we play hard. . . . And I tell you, it gets cold up there for our fans those last few games. That gets them all wound up, and they get us all wound up. . . . "
—Terry Bradshaw, SI, December 24–31, 1979

In practical terms the Pittsburgh that Bradshaw described, that Bradshaw *felt*, that Bradshaw tried so hard to understand, was already gone by 1979. The steel mills that once served as the engine of American industry, producing nearly 100 million tons during World War II alone, were mostly shuttered, reduced to skeletal remains along the rivers that wind their way through the valleys surrounding the city. It was the mills that once gave Pittsburgh not just its economic lifeblood but also its identity. Author James Parton described the city in 1868, in an oft-repeated phrase, as "hell with the lid taken off." More than half a century later H.L. Mencken wrote of a train trip through the coal and steel towns of Western Pennsylvania: "I am not speaking of mere filth. One expects steel towns to be dirty. What I allude to is the unbroken and agonizing ugliness, the sheer revolting monstrousness, of every house in sight. . . . "

This is the place in which the Steelers, then called the Pirates, were born in 1933, founded by Arthur Joseph Rooney, who would later be known as Art, or more lyrically, the Chief. Rooney was Pittsburgh to his core; he grew up on the North Side and ran the Steelers from their beginning until gradually handing them over to his son, Dan, beginning in the mid-1960s and formally in '75. (The Chief died in 1988 at the age of 87.) The Steelers didn't play a postseason game until 1947, when they and the Eagles finished 8–4, tied for first in the Eastern Division. The Steelers lost the conference playoff to the Eagles, 21–0.

The Steelers would not return to the postseason for a quarter century (excepting a 1962 appearance in the bizarre and short-lived Playoff Bowl, between conference second-place teams) but took solace in developing a reputation for leaving victorious opponents battered, fitting with the character of Mencken's Pittsburgh. "Hard-hitting, lovable losers," Joe Gordon, the longtime public relations director, described those old Steelers teams. "Every Monday the Chief would take back streets to work so he didn't run into any fans." This is a clever exaggeration—surely the Chief knew that the people of Pittsburgh, while longing for a winner, embraced the grit and physicality of the franchise.

Of those struggling Steelers teams, Cope wrote in 1973, "So you see, it was not that we always had the worst talent in the league. Heroes we always had. They thrived in the black pall that rose from the steel mills along the Monongahela; they perfected the brand of football the working people loved. From Johnny Blood to "Bullet" Bill Dudley to Bobby Layne and John Henry Johnson, we had football players to cheer, but usually not enough of them."

IN 1969 THE STEELERS MOVED TO AN ENTIRELY DIFFERENT path. They had been coached by 14 men in their first 36 seasons, not unusual for a team that struggled so badly. That would change abruptly. In that year of the moon landing and Woodstock and the Miracle Mets, Dan Rooney, just 36, wanted to hire rising Penn State coach Joe Paterno to lead the Steelers. Paterno chose to stay in State College, and so Rooney turned instead to a Baltimore Colts assistant named Chuck Noll. In the 43 years that followed, Pittsburgh has played in eight Super Bowls, winning six, and made the playoffs 26 times. The key to that sustained performance has been a bedrock, across-the-board stability that is nearly unprecedented in American sports and that mirrors precisely the attitude Bradshaw once described. It is a philosophy that a steelworker—or his descendants—could appreciate, long after the mills were gone.

In a league that churns through coaches like bark through a chipper, the Steelers have had just three since Noll was hired before that 1969 season. After 23 seasons, he was succeeded by Bill Cowher, who ruled the sideline for 15 seasons, from 1992 to 2006. Then Mike Tomlin took over. In a league in which teams change business models and football strategies to fit a high draft choice's skill set, the Steelers have consistently stressed punishing defense and shunned flash. They seldom signed big-money free agents or took risks on marginal personalities, a strategy that has solidified the bond between the franchise and its fans, themselves the product of a blue-collar culture rolling back multiple generations. And when a player has run afoul of this philosophy, as when quarterback

Ben Roethlisberger was accused of sexual assault, the citizenry turned sharply on him, demanding—and receiving—better behavior.

In a 2009 interview with SI, league commissioner Roger Goodell said, "One of the most critical elements in the success of the NFL is that a team takes on the character of its community. Nobody does that better than the Steelers. The team reflects the values of the community." That sentiment was echoed by Giants president and CEO John Mara, whose family has been close with the Rooneys through the

Noll, who reigned for 23 seasons, began a remarkable coaching run—the Steelers have had just three in more than four decades.

decades. (Actress Rooney Mara is the great-granddaughter both of Art Rooney and of Giants founder Tim Mara.) "Over the years you've seen Pittsburgh teams that are always tough and physical. The identity of the team is the identity of the city. I don't think that's an accident."

None of this escaped Dan Rooney. He learned stewardship from his father, and both are now enshrined in the Pro Football Hall of Fame. Dan, who played quarterback at Pittsburgh's North Catholic High, began attending Steelers games at Forbes Field with his mother when he was five years old. At 14 he was a ball boy in training camp, and in his mid-30s he was essentially running the team. It was Dan who oversaw the building of what evolved into the Noll dynasty. He would also become a powerful voice in the business of the modern NFL—so much that the league's mandate on interviewing minority candidates for head coaching vacancies is called the Rooney Rule. Said John Mara in 2009: "When Dan speaks at a league meeting, you can hear a pin drop in the room."

The expressive Cowher, who led the Black and Gold for 15 years, enjoyed his greatest success with Roethlisberger at quarterback.

Dan Rooney, who was born in 1932, developed a keen ability to move as a king or a commoner. In January 2009, having handed control of the Steelers to his son Art Rooney II, he attended a black-tie dinner in Washington on the eve of Barack Obama's presidential inauguration, and two months later he was named U.S. ambassador to Ireland. Throughout his tenure he was as likely to poke his head into the Steelers press room to trade stories with reporters and bloggers as he was to get on the phone

with Goodell or his fellow NFL power brokers. He often could be seen in the team cafeteria at mealtime, taking a tray and patiently standing in line. "Where else can you eat lunch every day with the owner?" veteran linebacker James Farrior once said. You could also see Rooney, mid-morning, tooling around the parking lot, looking for a spot.

All of this stems from Rooney's acute sense of his team's standing in the city of Pittsburgh. "In good times and bad times I've seen what this team means to the community," he said in January '09, before the Steelers' sixth Super Bowl victory. "When we win, the whole town is up. Doctors have told me that their patients feel better when we win. Pittsburgh is a diverse community, and we help to bring it all together. We have a responsibility to make sure we do things right."

They never did things more right than during the 1970s, when the city's love for the Steelers turned into a genuine passion. It was at the beginning of that run that Noll, Dan Rooney and Art Rooney Jr. (Dan's brother) established another rule that reflected the ideals of the city: They would build the team through the draft, slowly if necessary. The Steelers plumbed small colleges and historically black schools for talent that other teams might overlook. It began in Noll's first year, with three future bedrocks of the Super Bowl teams, and it's telling that all three were linemen: defensive tackle Joe Greene out of North Texas in the first round, tackle Jon Kolb from Oklahoma State in the third, and in the 10th round, the 238th pick of the 1969 draft, defensive end L.C. Greenwood, from Arkansas AM&N (now Arkansas-Pine Bluff). It helped to be a little lucky too—the following year the Steelers won a coin flip with the Bears for the first pick in the draft and the right to take the consensus No. 1, a strong-armed quarterback from Louisiana Tech named Terry Bradshaw. But savvy was evident as well that year: Fifty-two picks after Bradshaw, the Steelers tapped a rangy cornerback out of all-black Southern University, Mel Blount. They are the only two players from the 1970 draft to make the Hall of Fame.

The draft hits continued: Linebacker Jack Ham of Penn State was taken in 1971, and in '72 the Steelers, with the 13th overall pick, selected Nittany Lions running back Franco Harris when many thought they would take the player he blocked for at Penn State, All-America tailback Lydell Mitchell. Harris ended up outrushing Mitchell in the pros by nearly 6,000 yards and was the only Hall of Famer from that year's draft. Then in 1974 came the greatest draft by a single team in NFL history: receiver Lynn Swann of USC in the first round, linebacker Jack Lambert of Kent State in the second, wideout John Stallworth of Alabama A&M in the fourth and center Mike Webster of Wisconsin in the fifth. All four are enshrined in Canton. Pittsburgh also signed an undrafted safety out of South Carolina State that year: Donnie Shell. A three-time All-Pro who lasted 14 seasons, Shell was a finalist in the Hall of Fame voting in 2002 and a semifinalist in 2004.

THROUGHOUT THAT PERIOD AND BEYOND THE Steelers would not trade in desperation, and in later years they would pass up fancy free-agent signings. "Panic doesn't seem to work," Art II told *The New York Times* in February 2011, before the Steelers' eighth Super Bowl appearance, against the Packers. "Our philosophy is, you pick good people and try to stick with them. There's no guarantees. There are ups and downs in any sport. But if you have the people in place, you always have a chance to be successful."

The defense in the Noll years was called the Steel Curtain, with Greene up front and Lambert patrolling the middle. Those Steelers were cerebral, but also intimidating, in a time when football was a much rougher game than it would become decades later.

Bradshaw led the offense, throwing to Swann and Stallworth. Alongside Harris in the backfield was Rocky Bleier, a former Notre Dame star who had lost part of his right foot in Vietnam. It was a team that filled a void and captured a city. "A steelworker once said to me, 'As long as there's smoke up in the sky, I've got a job,'" said Rob Ruck, a Pittsburgh native and in 2009 a lecturer in history at the University of Pittsburgh. "Well, in the 1970s there was no smoke, and Pittsburgh, as a city, no longer had a job. It's impossible to overstate how Pittsburgh was battered by the collapse of the steel industry. The Steelers replaced that identity."

Twenty-six years would pass between the last Super Bowl title of the Noll dynasty, in the 1979 season, and the first under Cowher, in the 2005 season, Cowher's 14th and penultimate year at the helm. Bruising running back Jerome Bettis was the heart of that Super Bowl team, a jovial character who was as beloved in Pittsburgh as any member of the Steel Curtain squads. "As soon as you come here," said Bettis after his retirement, "you can sense that the franchise is revered in this city. And you know it was that way years and years before you came here. You don't find a lot of me-first players here. And it's not an accident. They don't target that type of player." Three years after Cowher's title, Tomlin would win his first championship.

As the NFL marches forward, each year reinforcing its unassailable position as America's most popular and lucrative league, it also now faces a dilemma: how to reconcile that popularity with the safety of its players, how to temper the violence on the field and reduce the hits that can lead to concussion or other serious damage. In 2010

that issue came to the forefront, and it was, appropriately, Steelers linebacker James Harrison who stood as the poster child for such violence—the type of hits upon which the Steelers' franchise was built—and the campaign against them. The team now walks a fine line while refusing to abandon its core practices.

Steelers history and heritage fairly spring from the seats on an autumn afternoon at Heinz Field. It is not uncommon in any sport to see the jerseys of long-gone players sprinkled among the crowd.

Tomlin, who like his two predeccessors was hired in his 30s, needed only two seasons to win his first Lombardi Trophy.

In Pittsburgh, though, it is particularly notable that you see BRAD-SHAW next to ROETHLISBERGER, GREENE next to HARRISON, STALLWORTH beside WARD. Forbes Field is gone, as is Pitt Stadium. Three Rivers, home to the great teams of the '70s, is no more. No steel mills line the rivers, no smoke clouds the sky. Time has changed, and the game has changed. But the Steelers remain vibrant, the beating heart of their city. ✦

STEE

The good guys wore black as the Steelers
took on the cold and the Jets in a
2003 game at the Meadowlands.

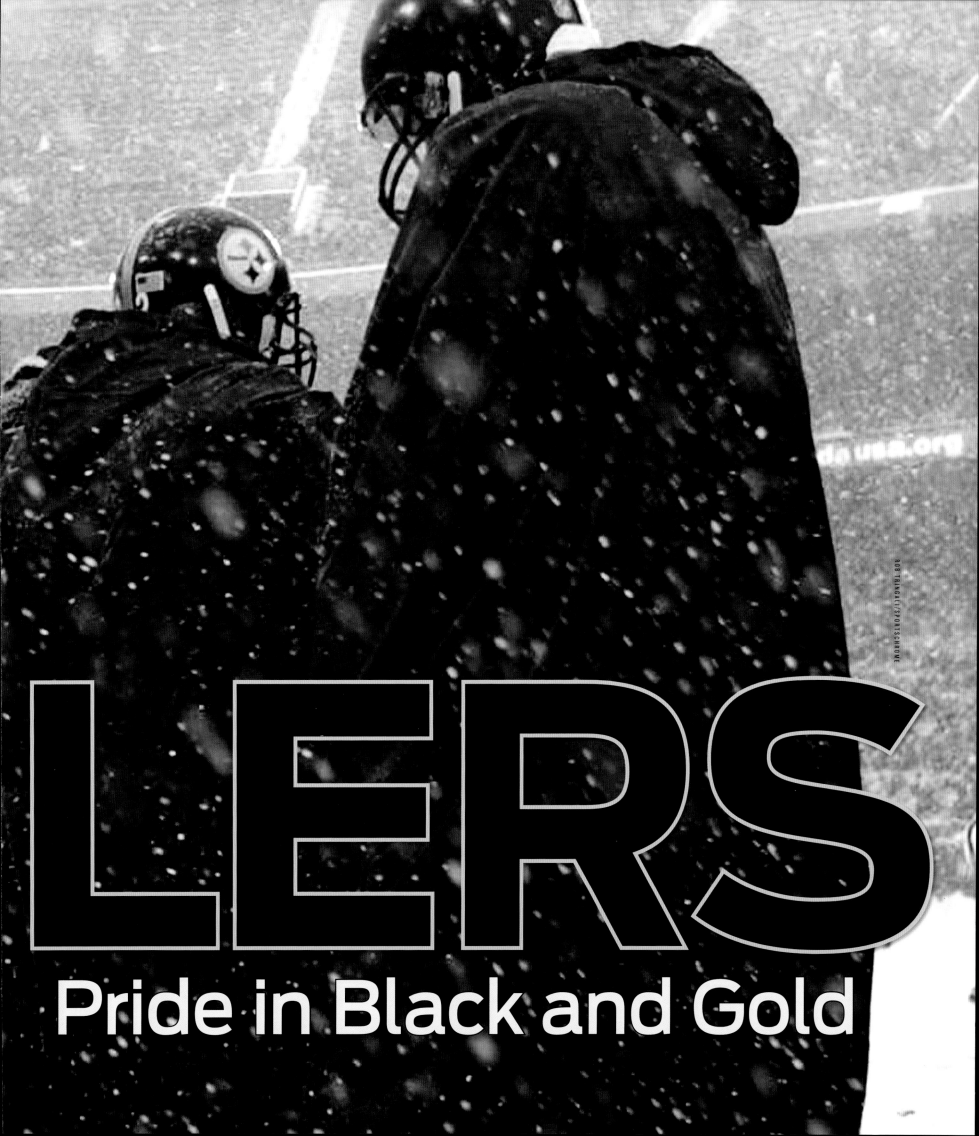

LERS

Pride in Black and Gold

THE PRIDE

The Steelers and their city have long understood that blue-collar and Black and Gold make a perfect match

WALTER IOOSS JR.

Terry Bradshaw and Willie Stargell, SI's co-Sportsmen of the Year in 1979, posed with workers at the Jones & Laughlin mill.

The semipro Pittsburgh Lyceum team of 1924, with Art Rooney (above, kneeling, far right), gave the city an early taste for football; servicemen in 1943 read about the Steagles—the combined Steelers-Eagles team that was cobbled together after the rosters of both franchises had been depleted by World War II (right); linebacker/guard John Reger (50) prowled the snow at Forbes Field in '60 (opposite).

PRO FOOTBALL HALL OF FAME/WIREIMAGE.COM; TEMPLE UNIVERSITY LIBRARIES URBAN ARCHIVES (SERVICEMEN); NEIL LEIFER (REGER)

> " [Our fans] lead a tough life, and they like a team with a tough defense. " —Terry Bradshaw

CLOCKWISE FROM LEFT: MORRIS BERMAN/WIREIMAGE.COM; HEINZ KLUETMEIER; HARRY CABLUCK/AP; COURTESY OF THE PITTSBURGH STEELERS

In the 1970s support for the Steelers, always strong, became a mania as the team began to collect titles. Franco Harris, whose mother was Italian, developed his own army of fans, which included the crowd at Three Rivers, Frank Sinatra (near right) and of course the inimitable quarterback.

Fans went wild after a 1979 playoff win against the Oilers (above), while Harris was mobbed following the Immaculate Reception game (left) and Lynn Swann showed off his style (below).

> " The identity of the team is the identity of the city. " —Giants CEO John Mara

How popular did the Steelers become? Roy Gerela, the *placekicker*, had a cheering section (above); Joe Greene made a Coke commercial–turned–pop culture touchstone (near right); and fans flocked to training camp in Latrobe in '82 (far right).

"As soon as you come here, you can sense that the franchise is revered in this city." —Jerome Bettis

CLOCKWISE FROM TOP LEFT: CAROLYN KASTER/AP; GENE J. PUSKAR/AP; JOHN BIEVER; NEAL LAUREN/REUTERS

James Harrison got a lift at the Super Bowl XL parade (above); the Bus inspired love (below); Nate Washington and Santonio Holmes jumped for joy in 2006 (right); and the Incline (opposite) said it all.

EXCERPTED FROM SPORTS ILLUSTRATED / JULY 30, 1979

True Tales of the Terrible Towel

It began as a simple radio gimmick, but the golden cloth quickly became the beloved symbol of the bond between team and town

BY **MYRON COPE**

NOT LONG AGO, DAN ROONEY, THE PRESIDENT of the Pittsburgh Steelers, handed me a copy of *Sports Business—The Management Newsletter for Sports Money Makers*. He pointed to an item he knew would interest me. Under the advisory "Watch for Fans," *Sports Business* confided to the moguls who subscribe to it: "Special, almost unclassifiable gimmicks like the Steelers' 'Terrible Towel' are a fan turn-on. The keys to the most successful of these devices seem to be 1) Color and 2) Motion. Crowds dressed in the same color clothing can make an impact, but it is passive. Color plus motion in the stands creates a kind of framework for the contest itself, making the entire experience more memorable for the spectator. We suggest a look at the Japanese and British sports crowds for examples of dynamic display of color and motion."

I, as the creator of the Terrible Towel, an instrument with which Steeler fans had flogged their team to victories in Super Bowls X and XIII (the Steelers somehow won Super Bowl IX without it), could not decide which impressed me more—*Sports Business*'s expertise in determining that color plus motion had made the towel a success, or my audacity in creating the towel while ignorant of the fact that I was mixing a precise formula that would produce a "special, almost unclassifiable gimmick."

During the NBC telecast of Super Bowl XIII, Curt Gowdy had referred to the towel as the "dirty towel," an allusion that did not especially annoy me inasmuch as Gowdy had botched the names of legions of professional football players. Let him know that *Sports Business*, which gets $60 for 24 issues from sports moneymakers, perceives the impact of the Terrible Towel, which, dirty or laundered, is held to be good reason for the moneymakers to take a close look at Japanese and British crowds. Lord, that I had known all that at the beginning!

"Your idea was pure genius," said Rooney. "But you were too stupid to know what you were doing."

Here I should explain that I am a Pittsburgh radio/television sports commentator and an analyst of Steelers games on radio. Late in November of 1975, I received a call from the secretary to the vice president and general manager of WTAE-Radio, who said, "Can you step over to Ted's office?" Crossing the hall, I found the burly figure of Ted J. Atkins. He was huddled with the vice president for sales, Larry Garrett. Atkins said,

Cope conceived of the towel in 1975, after a radio station executive asked him to come up with a way to celebrate the Steelers.

"The Steelers are going into the playoffs. As you know, the first game will be here in Pittsburgh. As the Steelers' flagship radio station, we think we should come up with some sort of gimmick that will involve the people."

Then Atkins barked, "Come up with a gimmick!"

"I am not a gimmick guy," I replied. "Never *have* been a gimmick guy."

"You don't understand," said Garrett. He explained that were I to promote some kind of object that the fans would wave or wear at the playoffs, advertisers would be so impressed by my hold on the public that they would clamor to sponsor my various shows.

"Besides," said Garrett, "your contract with us expires in three months."

"I'm a gimmick guy," I shrugged.

Advertising salesmen were hurriedly summoned to Atkins's office. Brainstorms erupted. "I've got it!" cried a salesman. "Chuck Noll's motto is 'Whatever it takes,' right?" Totally sober, the salesman proposed that we dress the 50,000 fans entering Three Rivers Stadium in black costume masks upon which Noll's motto would be printed in gold lettering. A phone call to a supplier of novelties revealed that 50,000 black masks could be obtained at a cost of 50¢ apiece, or $25,000. Vice presidents Atkins and Garrett incisively concluded that black masks were not the crowd-pleaser we were looking for.

"What we need here," I said to them, "is something that's lightweight and portable and already is owned by just about every fan."

"How about towels?" Garrett said.

"A towel?" It had possibilities. "We could call it the Terrible Towel," I said. "Yes. And I can go on radio and television proclaiming, 'The Terrible Towel is poised to strike!' "

"Gold and black towels, the colors of the Steelers," someone piped.

"No," I said. "Black won't provide color. We'll tell 'em to bring gold or yellow towels."

"Yellow and gold will fly!" cried a sales voice. "Tell 'em if they don't have one, buy one, and if they don't want to buy one, dye one!"

"I'll tell 'em they can use the towel to wipe their seats clean," I said. "They can use it as a muffler against the cold. They can drape it over their heads if it rains."

Another great concept in broadcasting having been born, Ted J. Atkins sent out for champagne. Later, when the Terrible Towel advanced for final

The towel was displayed by (from left) a tailgating fan before a 2011 playoff game, a rowdy guest in 1979, Sidney Crosby in 2006, and by pilots landing in Dallas for Super Bowl XLV.

approval to Franklin C. Snyder, vice president and general manager of the Hearst Broadcasting System, he ordered only one change. "We must have black towels too," he said gravely. "If we exclude black, we'll be asking for trouble from the Human Relations Commission and the FCC."

A few days later, on the heavily watched Sunday night 11 o'clock television news, I introduced Pittsburgh to the Terrible Towel, making a damned fool of myself by hurling towels at the anchorman, the weatherman and everyone else. Public response was instant and pleasantly flabbergasting. One of the few resisters was a co-captain of the Steelers, linebacker Andy Russell.

"What's this crap about a towel?" he growled at me in the locker room several days later. "We're not a gimmick team. We've never been a gimmick team."

His words had the ring of familiarity. But I fell back upon bravado. "Russell," I said, "you're sick."

Mind you, I did not see the Terrible Towel as witchcraft to hex the enemy. It would be a positive force, driving the Steelers to superhuman performance. Unsure of my own sanity, almost daily I intoned on radio and television, "The Terrible Towel is poised to strike!"

The very morning of the first playoff game, against Baltimore, the *Pittsburgh Post-Gazette* warned that I was trying to turn Three Rivers Stadium into a tenement neighborhood, yet at least 30,000 spectators turned up for the game waving Terrible Towels. It was a fine start. In foul, wet weather, wide receiver Frank Lewis wiped his hands with a Terrible Towel, then made a scarcely believable one handed catch of a Terry Bradshaw bullet. Later Bradshaw went down, his leg injured, and did not emerge from the locker room tunnel when his teammates took the field for the second half. Only seconds before play resumed, the crowd exploded, flailing the air with towels, for Bradshaw had reappeared.

Could Russell remain a nonbeliever? A young woman named Lisa Benz beheld the towel's effect upon him (Russell scooped up a Colts fumble and, though playing on an injured leg, lumbered 93 yards to a touchdown) and later mailed me the following verse.

> He ran ninety-three
> Like a bat out of hell,
> And no one could see
> How he rambled so well.
> "It was easy," said Andy,
> And he flashed a crooked smile,
> "I was snapped on the fanny
> By the Terrible Towel!"

Yea, verily did infidels cast aside their skepticism as the Steelers and the Terrible Towel whipped their way through the Oakland Raiders to the

American Conference title and through the Dallas Cowboys to victory in Super Bowl X.

Last year, Pittsburgh again earned home-field advantage for the playoffs. That dictated the Terrible Towel's resurrection, its use being reserved exclusively for postseason games. And if I may say so, this set a standard of commotion worthy of The Beatles and Elvis. The Denver Broncos came out on the field at Three Rivers and found themselves trapped in a vortex of yellow, gold and black terry cloth whirling against the bitter December sky like the swords of 50,000 Cossacks.

Next, Earl Campbell and the Houston Oilers came to town for the AFC Championship Game. Multitudes of western Pennsylvanians who had been unable to get tickets to the game draped towels over their television sets and radios, even over their dogs, cats and children. Towels hung from windows, lampposts and roofs. A department-store chain that offered Terrible Towels at $6.50 each, with a charity earmarked as the beneficiary, had run out of them in four hours;

The towel flies at Pittsburgh's zoo and airport (above) and also at the Magee-Womens Hospital of UPMC (right)—where infants don't have to endure being swaddled in pink or baby blue.

it then ordered another shipment and had run out in two hours.

But it was the Super Bowl showdown against the Dallas Cowboys at Miami that troubled me. "The Terrible Towel does not like to travel," I cautioned the faithful in my radio and television commentaries. "The towel breathes life from the support it gets from fans in the stadium, but Steeler fans are finding Super Bowl tickets hard to come by." Those fans, I had forgotten, had demonstrated at two previous Super Bowls involving their team that when it came to procuring tickets, John D. Rockefeller was no more adept at unearthing oil. They showed up in the Orange Bowl at least 20,000 strong, flying their Terrible Towels, and at game time the towel gave a sign to the nation that it was ready.

On the Steelers' first play from scrimmage, center Mike Webster hunkered over the ball wearing a yellow Terrible Towel tucked into his waistband. "I believe," said Bradshaw as he lined up over Webster. He touched the towel and proceeded to bombard the Cowboys dizzy, firing four touchdown passes. The Steelers were ahead by 18 points, with some

seven minutes remaining, when I trotted down from our booth to the Pittsburgh bench to be nearer the locker room, where I would conduct postgame radio interviews.

"Here," Webster said to me. He handed me the game towel, soggy by now. "I guess we don't need this anymore."

Mind you, being high priest of a towel does not turn my head. I have published four books and, before that, learned to play the clarinet, saxophone and piano. Yet it now appears certain that when my time comes, they will say of me in Pittsburgh, my lifelong home-town, "Oh, he was the fellow who had that towel." Indeed, in the aftermath of Super Bowl XIII, I received notification from the Pro Football Hall of Fame at Canton, Ohio, that a set of three Terrible Towels was to be enshrined there for all to behold. I must remember to visit the Hall of Fame to see if the towels hang alongside the busts of Bronko Nagurski and Sammy Baugh, or in a lavatory. Either way, I shall remain composed. ✦

Receiver Ron Shanklin (25) watched with defensive stars Blount (47), White (78), and Holmes (63) during Super Bowl IX.

THE PLAYERS

From John Henry Johnson to Troy Polamalu, what has made the Black and Gold special is the men who wore the colors

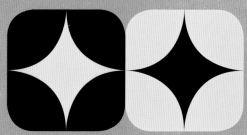

JEROME BETTIS

ROCKY BLEIER

TERRY BRADSHAW

DERMONTTI DAWSON

ALAN FANECA

FRANCO HARRIS

JOHN HENRY JOHNSON

BOBBY LAYNE

ELBIE NICKEL

BEN ROETHLISBERGER

JOHN STALLWORTH

LYNN SWANN

HINES WARD

MIKE WEBSTER

FENSE

Bradshaw (12) rolled out with Bleier (20) clearing a path against Oakland in the 1974 AFC title game; the 24–13 win sent Pittsburgh to its first Super Bowl.

JEROME BETTIS

**RUNNING BACK 1996–2005
SIX-TIME PRO BOWL SELECTION
EIGHT CAREER 1,000-YARD SEASONS**

THE JOVIAL JEROME BETTIS WAS ONE OF the most popular players in Steelers history, with a blue-collar nickname (The Bus) and dimensions (a Ralph Kramden–like 5' 11", 255 pounds), and a propensity for running over defenders as often as he ran around them. Acquired from the Rams in a 1996 trade, Bettis accumulated some of his biggest numbers in his early years in Pittsburgh—including a career-high 1,665 yards in '97—but his most memorable season was his last. That year he gained only 368 rushing yards (while scoring nine touchdowns) but ended his career in storybook fashion, playing his final game in his hometown of Detroit and walking out a champion as he helped the Steelers to defeat the Seahawks in Super Bowl XL. ✦

Bettis, who ran for 13,662 career yards, was named the league's Walter Payton Man of the Year in 2001 for his charitable work.

ROCKY BLEIER

RUNNING BACK 1968, 1971–80
25 CAREER TOUCHDOWNS
TOUCHDOWN CATCH IN SUPER BOWL XIII

H E IS ALONE AMONG STEELERS GREATS IN that he is the only one to author a SPORTS ILLUSTRATED cover story. Rocky Bleier left the Steelers after the 1968 season to serve in Vietnam, and in '75 he wrote for the magazine about his combat experiences—which included taking a bullet in the thigh. The injury earned him a Purple Heart, and also threatened to put an end to his football career.

But Bleier worked his way back onto the field and played a key role for four Super Bowl champions. It is easiest to remember him as a blocker, paving the way for backfield mate Franco Harris. But Bleier also excelled when carrying the ball himself, and in 1976 he rushed for a career-best 1,036 yards. ✦

In 1976 Bleier (left) and Harris became one of only six pairs of teammates ever to rush for 1,000 yards in the same season.

FROM LEFT: WALTER IOOSS JR.; HEINZ KLUETMEIER

TERRY BRADSHAW

QUARTERBACK 1970–1983
PRO FOOTBALL HALL OF FAME 1989
NFL MVP 1978

FROM LEFT: NEIL LEIFER; HEINZ KLUETMEIER

WHEN TERRY BRADSHAW WAS CHOSEN by the Steelers with the top overall pick in the 1970 draft, he was looked at as a potential savior for a franchise that had never known success. "We were desperate for anyone to turn us around," linebacker Andy Russell said. Bradshaw obviously didn't do it alone, and he had some bumpy early years, including a benching in '74, but there's little doubt that he was instrumental in transforming the franchise. The once-sorry Steelers morphed into perennial contenders, led on offense by a quarterback who could deliver big plays when needed. He once held records for TD passes in the postseason (30) and the Super Bowl (nine) and was twice awarded the Super Bowl MVP. ✦

Under the tutelage of coach Chuck Noll (above), Bradshaw twice led the NFL in touchdown passes, in 1978 and '82.

EXCERPTED FROM SPORTS ILLUSTRATED / DECEMBER 18, 1978

Li'l Abner Finally Makes It Big

How Terry Bradshaw, the smiling country boy
from Shreveport, learned to live in the spotlight
and lead the Steelers to the Super Bowl

BY RON FIMRITE

FOR A MAN THOUGHT BY THE GLIB AND THE uninformed to be simple, Terry Bradshaw has had a rather complex life. He was the first college player selected in the 1970 NFL draft, and he became, thereby, famous overnight. Nothing in his upbringing had prepared him for such recognition, and he squirmed in the limelight, a frightened and bewildered star. His country ways caused him to be too quickly characterized as an Ozark Ike type, and his Bible Belt philosophy made him appear more foolish than sincere among the supposedly sophisticated. He tried and failed to conceal his naiveté behind unnatural bravado, exposing himself to even more ridicule.

He has been married twice, to a beauty queen and an international ice-skating star. He has acted in a Hollywood movie (*Hooper*) opposite Burt Reynolds, and he enjoyed a brief, not entirely unsuccessful career as a country and western singer, a career he may well resume. Whatever he may become, now he is a football player who is having his best season, with a team-record 26 touchdown passes and 2,784 yards passing, and he is at long last earning his due as one of the game's finest quarterbacks.

Bradshaw led the Steelers to their first NFL championship, achieved by means of a 16–6 win over the Vikings in Super Bowl IX. The next year the Steelers repeated, defeating the Cowboys 21–17 in Super Bowl X. The decisive touchdown in that game came on a 64-yard Bradshaw-to-Lynn-Swann pass, a play called at the line of scrimmage when Bradshaw correctly detected Dallas in a safety blitz. He released the ball before he was hurled to the ground by a pack of Cowboys, and Swann caught it in open space. It was the sort of play-calling one expects from intellectual quarterbacks like Fran Tarkenton, Bob Griese or Ken Stabler. But Bradshaw?

Yes, he is a smart quarterback, his unfortunate image to the contrary. Although he has been picking NFL defenses to pieces all year, he remains, in the eyes of the ignorant, "dumb." Steelers coach Chuck Noll, who is as outwardly emotional as a throw rug, bristles at any suggestion that his quarterback reads defenses remedially. "That's ridiculous," he snaps. "People who say he's dumb should look in the mirror." Bradshaw calls all of his own plays, often brilliantly. Roger Staubach, supposedly a clever quarterback, calls almost none of his. When the 49ers foolishly tried to blitz Bradshaw in November, he deftly threw three touchdown passes. He engineered a masterly 11-play, 80-yard drive against Houston that transformed a bitter defensive struggle into a clear-cut Steelers victory. Bradshaw is exasperated and hurt by the slurs on his intelligence. "It is a thorn in my side, and it always will be," he says. "I could get a doctorate in chemical engineering and they'd call me dumb. If there is one thing I've learned about an image, it is that you can never get rid of it. I just can't fight it any longer. I have to live with it."

Bradshaw suspects he got his movie role because Reynolds, now a friend, felt guilty about calling him dumb on television. In their fight scene in *Hooper*, which required Bradshaw to hoist the actor off his feet and snarl insults at him, Bradshaw achieved a measure of revenge by ad-libbing, "Listen here, dummy. Aren't you ever going to learn?" ✦

People who said Terry Bradshaw wasn't smart probably didn't know that during all those huge wins he was calling his own plays.

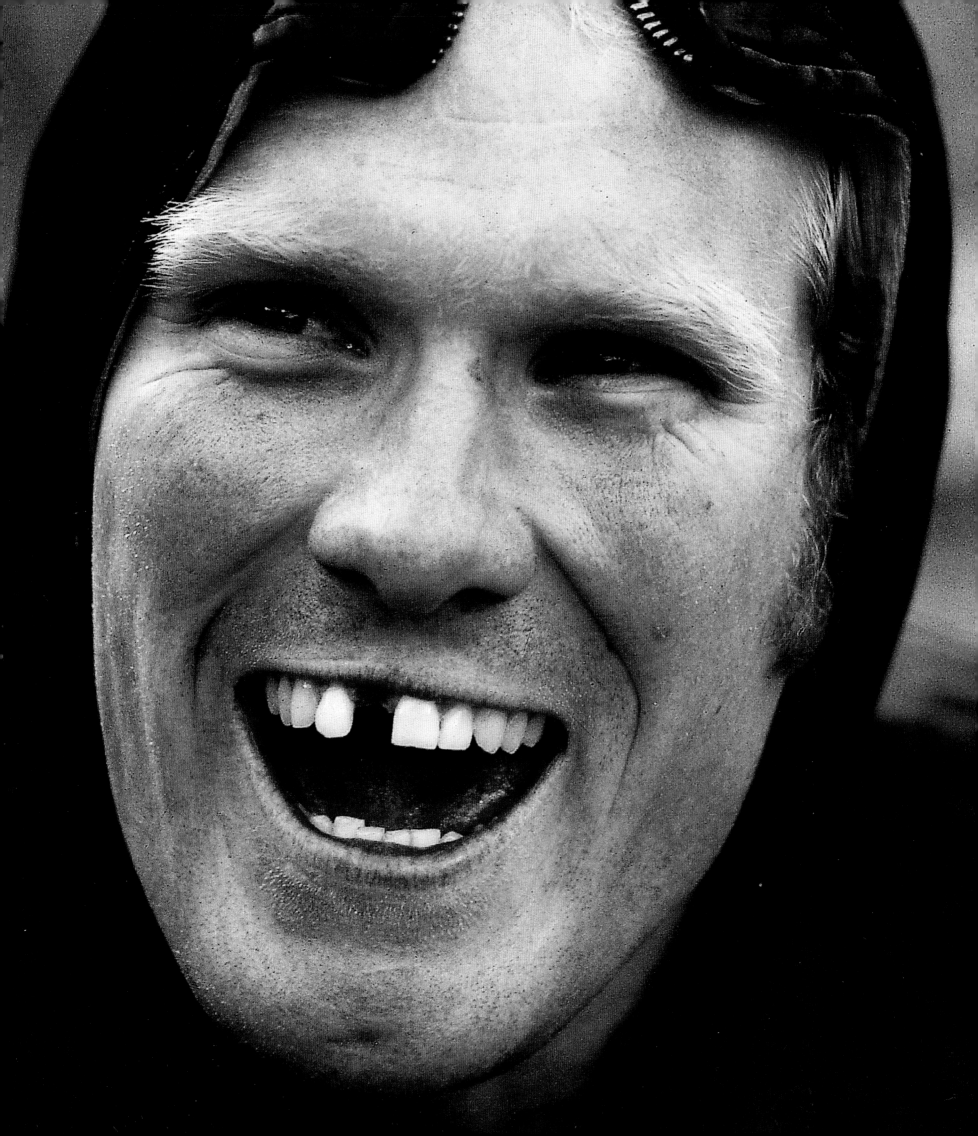

DERMONTTI DAWSON

CENTER 1988–2000
PRO FOOTBALL HALL OF FAME 2012
SIX-TIME ALL-PRO

ERMONTTI DAWSON WAS AS STRONG AND tough as a bull, but what really made him a superior offensive lineman was his speed. In 1989, his second season in Pittsburgh, he was moved from guard to center to take over from retiring Hall of Famer Mike Webster, and it could be argued that he actually provided an upgrade at the position. On running

Dawson (63), in addition to being strong and swift, was remarkably durable, playing in 170 consecutive games.

plays Dawson could get to defensive linemen so quickly that he did not need help from a guard to make his blocks after snapping the ball; more often it was the 6' 2", 288-pound Dawson coming to the aid of his linemates, freeing them up to attack defenders farther down the field. Running back Jerome Bettis, one of the prime beneficiaries of Dawson's talents, declared to SI in '98, "He's not the quickest center in the league, he's the quickest *lineman* in the league. He has the ability to snap the ball, pull and lead a sweep." In doing so Dawson redefined expectations about what a center could be. ✦

ALAN FANECA

GUARD 1998–2007
NFL 2000s ALL-DECADE TEAM
SIX-TIME ALL-PRO

WHEN THE OFFENSIVE LINE WAS opening holes for Jerome Bettis and Willie Parker, the quick and durable Alan Faneca was usually leading the charge. Though he left after the 2007 season to sign a rich contract with the Jets, the Louisiana native loved playing in the Burgh. In '06 he told SI the city's football passion was the NFL's version of the SEC frenzy he saw in college at LSU. "You'd never think you'd be able to have the following and enthusiasm you have with the Steelers fans," Faneca said. "People bleed black and gold. It's special." ✦

In Faneca's 10 seasons in Pittsburgh, the Steelers had a top 10 rushing attack nine times, including the No. 1 ranking in 2001.

FRANCO HARRIS

RUNNING BACK 1972–1983
PRO FOOTBALL HALL OF FAME 1990
STEELERS' ALLTIME RUSHING AND TD LEADER

T IS A HECK OF A RÉSUMÉ. FRANCO HARRIS WAS THE 1972 Rookie of the Year, the Super Bowl IX Most Valuable Player, the NFL's 1976 Man of the Year for his charitable work and, of course, the Immaculate Receiver, pulling in the ricocheted pass and scoring the touchdown against Oakland in the '72 playoffs that kick-started the Steelers' dynasty years. Critics noted that the thoughtful Harris often ran around tacklers rather than through them, but whatever the style—and at 6' 2" and 230 pounds he could bang with the best of them—he did it to great success: Harris had 47 100-yard games and at one point ranked behind only Jim Brown on the NFL's alltime rushing list. ✦

Harris delivered most when the stakes were highest, scoring 17 touchdowns and rushing for 1,556 yards in 19 postseason games.

JOHN HENRY JOHNSON

FULLBACK 1960–1965
PRO FOOTBALL HALL OF FAME 1987
STEELERS' FIRST 1,000-YARD RUSHER

A CLASSIC POWERHOUSE FULLBACK, John Henry Johnson would just as soon run over defenders as go around them. He initially earned recognition as a member of the 49ers' famed Million Dollar Backfield of the 1950s, but his most productive statistical years came after he had moved on to Pittsburgh. Bobby Layne loved having him in his backfield, declaring, "A quarterback hits the jackpot when he gets a combination runner-blocker like Johnson." He ran for more than 1,000 yards in both '62 and '64, and in six seasons he set a franchise career mark for rushing yards that stood until it was eclipsed by Franco Harris. ✦

Johnson (35) was a four-time Pro Bowl selection and scored 55 touchdowns while playing for four teams over 13 seasons.

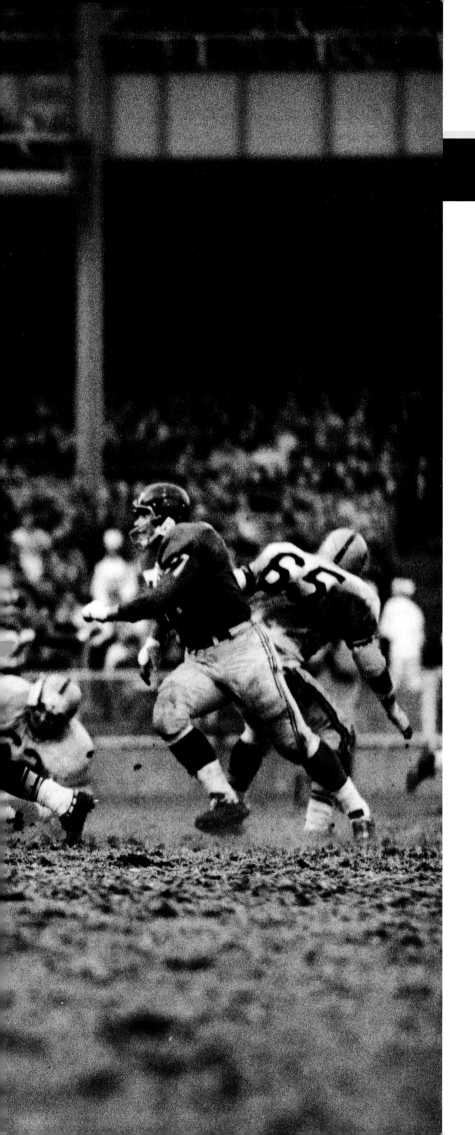

BOBBY LAYNE

QUARTERBACK 1958–1962
PRO FOOTBALL HALL OF FAME 1967
SIX-TIME CAREER PRO BOWL SELECTION

ACCORDING TO LEGEND THE THREE-TIME NFL champion had a parting shot for Detroit when it traded him to the Steelers early in the 1958 season: "The Lions won't win for the next 50 years." He was right and then some—Detroit has not even played for an NFL title since; in Motown they call it the Curse of Bobby Layne. In Pittsburgh the trade was more of a blessing as Layne—reunited with his old Lions coach, Buddy Parker—brought a winning attitude and some actual wins to a franchise that was desperate for them: Layne's tenure marked the Steelers' best five-year span until the 1970s. ✦

When Layne retired after 15 seasons in 1962 he was the NFL's career leader in passing touchdowns, yards and completions.

ELBIE NICKEL

**TIGHT END/DEFENSIVE END 1947–1957
THREE-TIME PRO BOWL SELECTION
FIFTH ALLTIME IN STEELERS RECEIVING YARDS**

WHEN ELBIE NICKEL DIED IN 2007, Dan Rooney rhapsodized that the tight end had made what was considered the most famous play in team history until the Immaculate Reception—Nickel's 52-yard touchdown catch that gave the Steelers a victory over the Eagles at Forbes Field in a hotly anticipated grudge match; the Eagles had broken quarterback Jim Finks's jaw in a game earlier in the season. Nickel was Pittsburgh's best pass-catcher through the franchise's early decades—his 329 receptions stood as a team record until Lynn Swann surpassed the mark in 1982. ✦

Nickel, who set a team record with 62 catches in 1953, was named to the Steelers' 75th anniversary team in 2007.

FROM LEFT: COURTESY OF THE PITTSBURGH STEELERS; PRO FOOTBALL HALL OF FAME

BEN ROETHLISBERGER

QUARTERBACK 2004–PRESENT
YOUNGEST STARTING QB TO WIN SUPER BOWL
NFL RECORD FOR WINS IN FIRST FIVE SEASONS

H IS CAREER BEGAN WITH A 13-GAME winning streak in his rookie season and a Super Bowl ring in his sophomore campaign. Back then, Ben Roethlisberger played quarterback conservatively as the Steelers relied on defense and the running game—their lone touchdown pass in Super Bowl XL was thrown by receiver Antwaan Randle El on a reverse. But by the time Big Ben led the Steelers to victory in Super Bowl XLIII he was commanding a spread passing attack and extending plays with his escapes from the pocket. It's the rare player who has so much success so early, and then goes on to become much better. ✦

FROM LEFT: HEINZ KLUETMEIER; MICHAEL J. LEBRECHT II//IDEUCE3 PHOTOGRAPHY

Numbers don't lie: In addition to two rings, Roethlisberger also owns the six highest quarterback season ratings in Steelers history.

JOHN STALLWORTH

WIDE RECEIVER 1974–1987
PRO FOOTBALL HALL OF FAME 2002
FOUR-TIME PRO BOWL SELECTION

W HATEVER HIS SUCCESSES IN THE regular season, John Stallworth defined his career in the playoffs. He caught 12 postseason touchdowns, the longest being a 75-yarder against Dallas in Super Bowl XIII. In the following Super Bowl he came back with an even greater highlight-reel play, a 73-yard score against the Rams that gave Pittsburgh a lead it never relinquished.

While the businesslike speedster was occasionally overshadowed by the charismatic Lynn Swann, it was Stallworth who accumulated greater numbers. Together they were as good a receiving tandem as the league has ever seen. ✦

On his retirement Stallworth held team records for receiving yards (8,723), receptions (573) and touchdowns (63).

LYNN SWANN

WIDE RECEIVER 1974–1982
PRO FOOTBALL HALL OF FAME 2001
MVP OF SUPER BOWL X

F STEELERS FOOTBALL IN THE 1970S WAS A cacaphony of hits, Lynn Swann provided the grace notes, punctuating the biker rally with moments of ballet. As a rookie he set a club record for punt return yards; soon Swann advanced to the starting lineup, making three Pro Bowls and playing his best on the biggest stage. In his four Super Bowls he caught 16 passes for 364 yards (still second most alltime) and three TDs. Super Bowl X was his showcase—his diving, acrobatic second-quarter catch made a memorable SI cover, and his fourth-quarter bomb from Terry Bradshaw proved the game-winner. ✦

Swann's touchdown catch (left) at Oakland in the 1974 AFC title game was a harbinger of many postseason heroics to come.

HINES WARD

WIDE RECEIVER 1998–2011
ALLTIME STEELERS LEADER IN RECEPTIONS
MVP OF SUPER BOWL XL

H E IS THE FIRST STEELER EVER TO CATCH 1,000 passes, and his career highlight may have been his game-sealing touchdown catch against Seattle in Super Bowl XL, but what ultimately defines Hines Ward is the unusual relish with which he delivered a block: He dived into the dirty work of his position with the gusto of a pulling guard. "Hines is not just blocking—he's knocking people's heads off, and he's making the defender look around, and that opens up the run game," Ben Roethlisberger told SI in 2006. In an era when many top wideouts cultivated a diva image, it fits with the Black and Gold tradition that the best Steelers receiver of his time distinguished himself by his toughness. ✦

The ever-cheerful Ward topped 1,000 yards six times, including in 2002, when he set a franchise mark with 112 receptions.

JOHN BIEVER (2)

MIKE WEBSTER

CENTER 1974–1988
PRO FOOTBALL HALL OF FAME 1997
NFL 75TH ANNIVERSARY TEAM

BOTH TOUGH AND TECHNICALLY SKILLED, Mike Webster was the Steelers' offensive captain for nine seasons. The five-time All-Pro was also a refreshingly humble team player. "After I'd interview him, he'd thank me, then smile and point to the crowded section of the locker room and say, 'Better go talk to the superstars,' " SI's Paul Zimmerman recalled in writing Webster's obituary after the lineman's death in 2002 at age 50. "In his mind he was just a workingman who played center. Many people feel no one ever played it better." ✦

The relentless and reliable Webster played in 177 consecutive games and 220 overall for the Steelers, both franchise records.

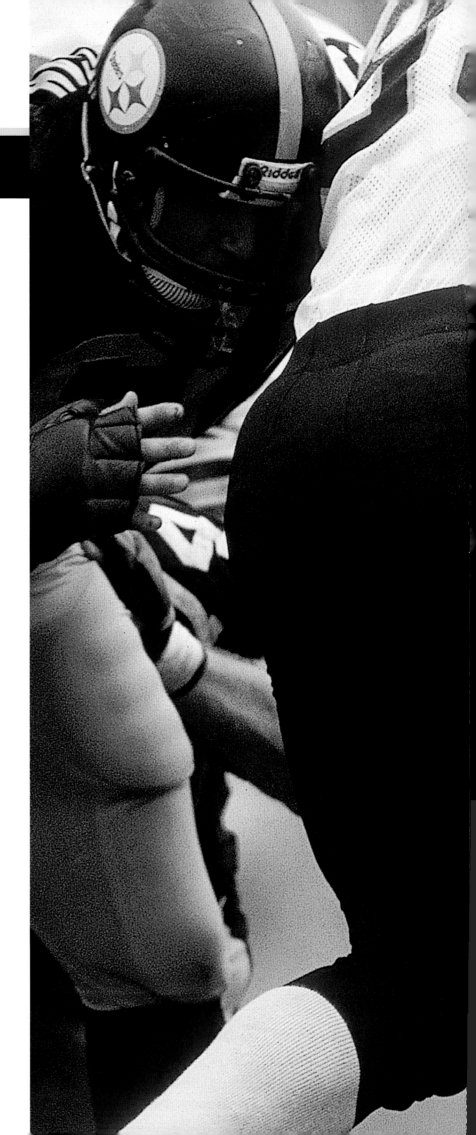

MEL BLOUNT

JACK BUTLER

JOE GREENE

L.C. GREENWOOD

JACK HAM

CASEY HAMPTON

JAMES HARRISON

ERNIE HOLMES

CARNELL LAKE

JACK LAMBERT

TROY POLAMALU

ANDY RUSSELL

AARON SMITH

ERNIE STAUTNER

DWIGHT WHITE

ROD WOODSON

DE

FENSE

Running was often futile against a front seven that included Greene (75), White (78), Holmes (63), Greenwood (68) and Lambert (58).

HEINZ KLUETMEIER

MEL BLOUNT

CORNERBACK 1970–1983
PRO FOOTBALL HALL OF FAME 1989
NFL 75TH ANNIVERSARY TEAM

WHAT JOE GREENE WAS TO THE front four and Jack Lambert was the linebacking corps, Mel Blount was to the secondary of the Steel Curtain defenses: a dominating physical force that set the tone for his unit. Blount's physicality was backed with a rare combination of size and speed. "The most Olympian sports body I've ever seen belongs to Wilt Chamberlain. . . . Mel has the same body, only scaled down from 7' 1" to 6' 3" "—wrote Roy Blount Jr. (no relation) in SI in 1983. Blount, the writer, further added, "In the Steelers' most dominant NFL years their bedrock strength was that they whipped people down into the dirt physically, and Blount was as big a part of that tradition as a defensive back can be."

If it is hard to imagine today's coverage-specialist cornerbacks intimidating in that manner—or standing 6' 3", it is in part because of a rule change that Blount is credited with inspiring. In 1978 the NFL began placing limits on the bump-and-run coverage at which Blount excelled, dictating that corners could no longer physically harass a receiver more than five yards past the line of scrimmage. This change opened the door to the pass-oriented offenses of the modern era. Blount, though, was skilled enough to adjust and thrive under the new rules. He made All-Pro for the fourth time in 1981. ✦

Blount intercepted a franchise-record 57 passes in his 14 seasons in Pittsburgh, including a league-leading 11 in 1975.

JACK BUTLER

CORNERBACK 1951–59
PRO FOOTBALL HALL OF FAME 2012
NFL 50TH ANNIVERSARY TEAM

JACK BUTLER LEFT SEMINARY SCHOOL AND found his calling in the Steelers' secondary. Undrafted out of St. Bonaventure, where he was an end on both offense and defense, Butler played mostly at cornerback for the Steelers, and he put the skills from his previous positions to good use. Butler was an exceptional tackler—Art Rooney Jr. called him the toughest player he ever saw—and a first-rate ballhawk: In 1957 he led the league with 10 interceptions. The Pittsburgh native was named All-Pro three straight years until a devastating knee injury cut short his career. In retirement he ran the BLESTO scouting service for more than four decades. ✦

FROM LEFT: BETTMANN/CORBIS; COURTESY OF THE PITTSBURGH STEELERS

Butler (80) played some receiver but made better use of his good hands on defense, intercepting 52 passes in his career.

JOE GREENE

DEFENSIVE TACKLE 1969–1981
PRO FOOTBALL HALL OF FAME 1987
NFL 75TH ANNIVERSARY TEAM

H E WAS CHUCK NOLL'S FIRST-EVER DRAFT pick, a first-rounder in 1969, and coming from tiny North Texas State not a particularly popular one—until fans saw him play. In a late-season game against the Oilers in 1972, the Steelers needed a win to make the playoffs for the first time. The defense was missing several players because of injury and the flu, but Joe Greene carried the day: He sacked the quarterback five times, blocked a field goal and forced and recovered a fumble. Pittsburgh was in, and Mean Joe (who wasn't really so mean) established himself as a man who could take over games, a reputation that would only grow as the Super Bowl rings accumulated. ✦

From his angled stance over the center, the two-time defensive player of the year dominated the middle and terrorized QBs.

FROM LEFT: NEIL LEIFER; JOHN IACONO

EXCERPTED FROM SPORTS ILLUSTRATED / SEPTEMBER 22, 1975

He Does What He Wants

He is called Mean Joe Greene, but he's really a nice guy—just ask all the people who are terrified of making him angry

BY **ROY BLOUNT JR.**

LIKE KATHARINE HEPBURN, CHARLES EDWARD (Mean Joe) Greene refuses to sign autographs. Like Bruce Lee, he kicks people. Like Winston Churchill, he cries. "I never had a desire to hurt anybody," Greene says. "I have at certain times had violent urges, but I don't think I ever have hurt anybody. Tried to a couple times, but I don't think I have. Yeah, guess I have. In high school. I was dirty then. Kick 'em. I might not've hurt 'em, though, they might've just been afraid of me.

"I do play football no-holds-barred. Any edge I can get, I'll take. I'd grab a face mask only in a fit of anger. Uncontrolled anger is damn near insane."

Greene once shattered three or four of Cleveland guard Bob DeMarco's teeth, and they were big teeth way back deep in the jaw. Once, Greene admits, he tried to twist the head off a fellow professional who was holding him. Is it because deep down inside they are so relieved that he is not going to twist their heads off—is that why people who spend time with him are proud to say that Joe Greene is a nice, warm, thoughtful, sensitive man?

Certainly there are other men who are nice and don't get the credit for it that Greene does. He's famous, that's part of it: He's the great defensive tackle and volatile cornerstone of the Super Bowl champion Pittsburgh Steelers. And he has such *bearing*. He may be the most nearly rollicking player in the NFL, but his expression, which can be affable, droll, quirky, smoldering, tends to settle into a basic grave. He can look as grave around the eyes as James Mason, but stronger, of course. His head may be as big as Mason's chest. Art Rooney Jr. says that Greene is the only man in whose mouth one of Steelers patriarch Art Rooney's huge billy-stick cigars looks normal.

No one would take Greene for a sweet/terrifying child of nature, the way they took the late Big Daddy Lipscomb. Greene has this *discerning* look. When Steelers quarterback Terry Bradshaw tells a joke to the team, one observer notes, he looks to Greene to see if it has gone over. If it's a good joke, it probably has. With teammates or friends, though not with fans, Greene is usually comfortable to be around. He doesn't dominate a table.

But there is that big head. And hands about the size of shovel blades.

Steelers center Ray Mansfield said of Greene, "If Joe really wants to shuck a guy . . . did you ever see a dog get hold of a snake?"

And there is a molten quality about Greene's limbs. He is no Apollo (Zeus, maybe). He is jointed oddly, and moves at once more smoothly and more floppily than other strong big men. His physical presence suggests, perhaps, that he could shift—*flick*—any loglike portion of himself in any direction at any moment. His college coach called him "a fort on foot." And sometimes, on the field, he goes damn near insane.

Wearing a loose T-shirt and a swimsuit, Greene sits back in a soft chair in his comfortable home in a suburb south of Dallas, with his two-year-old daughter Jo Quel drowsing on his chest. He has an air of profoundly edgy repose, like a mountain that would like to rumble but is not about to slide. He muses, "I'm always nervous like I got to do something, something other than what I'm doing. I don't know what it is. Except playing. When you get into that game, you haven't got time to think about what you ought to be doing. That game, that's it. I feel I've got some helluva games in me. I'm just waiting for 'em to come. That's what I keep pushing for—waiting."

Lord preserve our sense of reality if whatever consummation Greene awaits comes to him. The ground may open and he will descend to a place more intense, where he can chase Beelzebub around kicking at him, or a chariot may come down and bear Greene off to a better place where he can make all the tackles and also run back punts. As it is, Greene has led his team to the NFL mountaintop and has had transcendent individual moments on the field. Once he threw the other team's ball away. Once he spit on Dick Butkus in front of everybody. Once he rushed the quarterback, stole the ball from him, rumbled into the end zone with it, tossed it over his head, caught it behind his back and handed it to a cheerleader.

Greene is more than mighty, wily, fierce and twinkle quick. He is a man so daringly self-defined and outrageously responsible that it is said of him, as of very few other sports figures, "He does what he wants to out there." He plays—or, sometimes, refuses to play—the conservative, regimented, technology-ridden game of pro football as if it were a combat poem he is writing, and gets away with it, and yet fits himself well enough into the prevailing system to be the warmly accepted spearhead and bulwark of a winning organization. There is no ballad of Mean Joe Greene but there was a TV commercial. In this commercial Greene took a seat in a United Airlines plane, shifted his loosely put-together frame around to test the seat's comfort, then looked coldly, perhaps grimly, into the camera's eye and said, "I almost like it." ✦

L.C. GREENWOOD

DEFENSIVE END 1969–1981
TWO-TIME ALL-PRO
SIX-TIME PRO BOWL SELECTION

THE STEELERS SHOWED UNCANNY DRAFT acumen in building their 1970s Super Bowl teams, and there may be no better example than L.C. Greenwood, plucked out of Arkansas-AM&N (now Pine Bluff) in the 10th round in '69. This pillar of the Steel Curtain, who wore gold shoes while his teammates wore black, led the Steelers in sacks six times. Despite his achievements the Hall of Fame has eluded Greenwood, who's been a finalist six times, most recently in 2006. His largest problem may be that nine of his teammates have already been voted in; the abundance of Steelers could keep the native of Canton, Miss., from ever being enshrined in Canton, Ohio. ✦

Greenwood sacked Roger Staubach three times in Super Bowl X and harried him further in a 14–3 win at Three Rivers (left) in '79.

HEINZ KLUETMEIER (2)

JACK HAM

LINEBACKER 1971–1982
PRO FOOTBALL HALL OF FAME 1988
NFL 75TH ANNIVERSARY TEAM

F OR HIS FIRST GAME AT THREE RIVERS, JACK HAM had to talk his way past a guard who did not believe the scrawny kid from Johnstown, Pa., was a Steeler. But from that first day he proved he belonged, starting every game of his rookie season and quickly distinguishing himself with his intelligence and sense of where a play was going. The product of Linebacker U at Penn State also possessed one of the great football monikers ever, and though his meaty surname had little in common with his heady and agile style, his fan club was nonetheless named *Dobre Shunka*, Polish for "Good Ham." Every year they would reward their favorite outside linebacker by giving him one. ✦

Ham, a six-time All-Pro and eight-time Pro Bowl pick, had 32 interceptions and 25½ sacks in his storied 12-year career.

CASEY HAMPTON

NOSETACKLE 2001–PRESENT
FIVE-TIME PRO BOWL SELECTION
NAMED TO STEELERS' 75TH ANNIVERSARY TEAM

FROM LEFT: JOHN BIEVER; BILL FRAKES

HOW MUCH DOES CASEY HAMPTON *REALLY* weigh? He wouldn't tell an SI writer working on a 2011 story about the game's best defensive tackles, but he would allow that his media guide weight of 325 pounds was low. "Big men do not want you to know their real weight," he said. But the numbers that define Hampton's true worth are these: In nine of his first 10 seasons the Steelers were in the top three in the NFL in run defense, including four years in which they ranked first overall. Credit the big man in the middle for disrupting blocking schemes and making life hard for running backs searching desperately for daylight. ✦

Hampton (corralling Cincinnati's Bernard Scott, left) became an immediate starter after being drafted in the first round in 2001.

JAMES HARRISON

LINEBACKER 2002, 2004–PRESENT
TWO-TIME ALL-PRO
2008 DEFENSIVE PLAYER OF THE YEAR

O F THE SIX STEELERS TO BE NAMED NFL defensive player of the year, Harrison is the most unlikely. He went undrafted out of Kent State in 2002, then bounced between the practice squad, unemployment, special teams and stints with the Ravens and NFL Europe. Not until '07 did he become a regular starter and blossom into a leaguewide terror. Harrison certainly plays like a man who doesn't take his next play for granted. "If there's something that you say that I can't do," he told SI in '09, "I'm going to do everything between heaven and hell to prove you wrong." ✦

The hard-hitting Harrison, a four-time Pro Bowl selection, set a Steelers single-season mark with 16 sacks in 2008.

ERNIE HOLMES

DEFENSIVE TACKLE 1972–1977
TWO-TIME SUPER BOWL STARTER
40 CAREER SACKS

O N A TEAM OF INTIMIDATORS, NO ONE took a back seat to Ernie Holmes. So massive he needed two nicknames—Arrowhead and Fats—Holmes played with violence and anger, whether crashing into ballcarriers or getting in the face of Raiders' offensive lineman Gene Upshaw during warmups before the AFC Championship Game in 1976. In SI Roy Blount Jr. wrote of attending the Steelers' first Super Bowl celebration party: "I was reminded of how unsettling Holmes looks when I said to two different people, 'That's Ernie Holmes over there, you want to meet him?' and each of them said, 'Oh, my God.' " ✦

The arrow that Holmes (63), a.k.a. Fats, had shaved into his head completed the picture of a man following his own compass.

FROM LEFT: HEINZ KLUETMEIER; JOHN BIEVER

CARNELL LAKE

DEFENSIVE BACK 1989–1998
NFL 1990s ALL-DECADE TEAM
FIVE-TIME PRO BOWL SELECTION

CARNELL LAKE WAS A SUPERIOR ATHLETE with an equally strong attitude, as evidenced by how he seamlessly switched positions in the secondary when injuries to teammates required it. Players usually move from cornerback to safety, not the other way around as Lake did in 1995 and again in '97. "Carnell is as team-oriented a player as you'll find," coach Bill Cowher told SI in '98. "His best position is strong safety, but out of need he spent two years at corner for us. One time we went to the Super Bowl, the other time we went to the AFC Championship Game." Can't argue with the results. ✦

An All-Pro in 1997, Lake was outstanding in both tackling and coverage, finishing his career with 25 sacks and 16 interceptions.

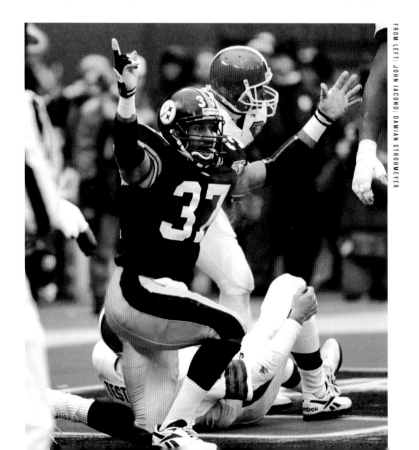

FROM LEFT: JOHN IACONO; DAMIAN STROHMEYER

JACK LAMBERT

LINEBACKER 1974–1984
PRO FOOTBALL HALL OF FAME 1990
NFL 75TH ANNIVERSARY TEAM

AT 218 POUNDS, JACK LAMBERT WAS relatively light for a middle linebacker. "I give away 20 pounds every time I step on the field," he once said, "so I have to be 20 pounds more aggressive." While Lambert's image is defined by the punishment he inflicted, the two-time Defensive Player of the Year also won with intelligence, calling the plays for coordinator Bud Carson's 4–3 defense. He was a Rookie of the Year, an eight-time All-Pro and the Steelers' defensive captain for eight seasons—and on a team stocked so heavily with Hall of Famers and outsized personalities, that last designation may be the most impressive accolade of all. ✦

FROM LEFT: NEIL LEIFER; WALTER IOOSS JR.

Lambert had 28 interceptions, 17 fumble recoveries and countless savage hits, including this one on the Colts' Lydell Mitchell.

EXCERPTED FROM SPORTS ILLUSTRATED / JULY 12, 1976

Meet Smilin' Jack

Pittsburgh's young middle linebacker plays with a vicious intensity that makes him stand out, even on a team of stars

BY ROBERT F. JONES

AS THE CLOSEST THING TO COMBAT IN civilian life, professional football is a breeding ground of legends that echo our rapidly fading warrior past. Reputedly the fiercest of these nascent legendary figures is Jack Lambert, the All-Pro middle linebacker of the Pittsburgh Steelers who after only two years in the NFL wears two Super Bowl rings on his fingers. According to Lambert's teammates and adversaries, he's the Grendel of the Gridiron, a cleated and bone-crunching blend of Caligula and King Kong who delights in snatching the soft parts from hapless backs and receivers and who performs open-heart surgery on the enemy using naught but his snaggled, bloody fingernails in lieu of a scalpel. He's not just meaner than mean. He's meaner than Greene!

"Jack Lambert is so mean," says Pittsburgh defensive tackle Mean Joe Greene, a legend in his own right, "that he don't even like *himself*."

He is a hard, quick hitter with a Sidewinder missile's instinct for the heat of action that puts him in the thick of the pileups on nearly every running play, yet with the speed and agility to cover halfbacks and even wide receivers on pass plays, both deep and shallow. During Super Bowl X in Miami last January, Lambert ran stride for stride with Dallas's Preston Pearson on one deep pattern and batted the ball away from a sure touchdown. On another occasion—and this is where the legend-makers' day was made—he picked up Cowboy safety Cliff Harris by the shoulder pads and "bench-pressed" him straight into the ground. Even when he wasn't on the field playing defense, Lambert was hopping on the sidelines like an animated pogo stick, huffing and puffing through his gapped front teeth, eyes rolling madly, exhorting his teammates on offense and howling invective at the Cowboys.

"People tell me that I get a little bit carried away during a game," Lambert allows with a farm-boy laconicism that betrays his rural roots. "I really don't remember it. I do remember the Harris incident, though. What happened was that our kicker, Roy Gerela, had missed a field goal, and Harris came running up to him, clapped both hands on Roy's helmet and said, 'Nice going. That really helps us.' Well, we were getting intimidated there in the first half and, I mean, we are supposed to be the intimidators. We couldn't have that. So I just grabbed Harris by the pads and flung him down. After the game the Cowboys said I was hitting late, taking cheap shots. That's

bunk. That's sour grapes. I hit hard, all right, but I hit fair. That's the name of the game." And, thanks in large measure to Lambert's kamikaze élan, it also spelled the final score: Steelers 21, Cowboys 17.

Needless to say, Lambert's teammates are among his most ardent fans. The greatest compliment comes from Mean Joe himself. "He's our spark, our spearhead," Greene says. "If I was ever in a barroom brawl and needed someone to go back-to-back with me, I'd want Jack Lambert to be the man."

A small-town kid from Mantua, Ohio (pop. 1,199), who spent summers pitching hay and slopping hogs on his grandfather's farm, Lambert was not particularly outstanding back when he was a 6' 4", 185-pound quarterback on the Crestwood High School football team. "I was mainly a hand-offer," Lambert recalls of his Crestwood quarterbacking days, "and my best time for the 40 back then was six seconds flat. When we flip-flopped, though, I played defensive halfback, and even then I loved to hit. Loved it." Nonetheless, only one Big Ten school—Wisconsin—showed any interest in him, and at one point Lambert thought of seeking a basketball scholarship. Instead, he enrolled at Kent State University, where he rapidly honed his skills and put on much-needed muscle, at middle linebacker. Today he plays at 218 pounds and can run the 40 in 4.7 seconds, excellent speed for a sockdolager.

One Pittsburgh sportswriter has called Lambert "the Nureyev of linebackers," a clear reference to his ability and balance in the middle of muddle.

"Who's Nureyev?" Lambert asks, deadpan again. The ballet dancer is defined for him.

"I don't know if that's a compliment or an insult," he says. "But I guess those guys are pretty good athletes, whatever else they do. I'll take it as a compliment."

Other old-time Steeler fans liken Lambert to the tough players of the team's early, losing years—men like Ernie Stautner and Bobby Layne, who hurt you when they played you, win or lose. "I like that comparison better," Lambert says. "That's what I'd really have liked, to play back in those days even though the money was hardly there. They played for the game—and to hit. Cripes, 50 bucks a game, but they loved it." ✦

"Jack Lambert is so mean," Mean Joe Greene once legendarily said of his teammate, "that he don't even like himself."

TROY POLAMALU

SAFETY 2003–PRESENT
FOUR-TIME ALL-PRO
2010 DEFENSIVE PLAYER OF THE YEAR

FROM LEFT: DAMIAN STROHMEYER; DAVID E. KLUTHO

IN BREAKING DOWN THE 2003 STEELERS, A SCOUT told SI that he loved the drafting of Troy Polamalu out of USC in the first round: "His physical play should make receivers nervous when they go over the middle." The assessment was only inaccurate in that it didn't go far enough. Before too long Polamalu was making opponents nervous everywhere—in the middle, on the outside, downfield, near the line of scrimmage and in their dreams. And it wasn't just receivers who feared seeing Polamalu's mop of thick black hair coming at them, but running backs and quarterbacks too. From pass rushing to coverage, he can line up anywhere and do anything, and that is what makes him such a rare force.   ✦

"If you don't know where he is, he'll kill you," New England coach Bill Belichick said of Polamalu, here tackling receiver Wes Welker.

EXCERPTED FROM SPORTS ILLUSTRATED / JANUARY 17, 2011

Like a Bolt of Pure Energy

Unpredictable Steelers safety Troy Polamalu is a freelancing force who can change a game with a single electrifying play

BY **TIM LAYDEN**

FOOTBALL IS WIDELY RULED BY TECHNICIANS, killjoys and personality police. But artists emerge, and they play the game as if it were jazz and not math. Joe Namath was an artist standing in the pocket, with white shoes and a quick release. Dick Butkus was an artist in pursuit of mayhem, forearms at the ready. Barry Sanders was an artist working in tight space, like liquid on cleats. They executed, but they also entertained. Troy Polamalu, the eighth-year strong safety of the Pittsburgh Steelers, is their descendant, turning defense into a form of expressionism.

Late on Saturday afternoon at Heinz Field in Pittsburgh, the Steelers will open their playoff run by hosting their bitter rivals, the Ravens. The 29-year-old Polamalu will be the most dynamic player on the field. He will blitz from the line of scrimmage, defend passes 50 yards into the secondary and tackle running backs from sideline to sideline.

Polamalu will do all of this in a frantic and unpredictable manner, as if he were playing a sandlot game with friends. "I never know where Troy is going to be lined up," says Steelers linebacker James Farrior. Says Rodney Harrison, former All-Pro safety and current NBC analyst, "There's no defensive player in the history of the NFL who has had the freedom Troy Polamalu has right now."

The Steelers drafted Polamalu with the 16th pick in 2003. As a young player he attacked hard and was frequently burned. "Teams used it against him," says Kennedy Pola, Polamalu's uncle and a longtime college and NFL coach. "His second year, AFC Championship against New England: pretty ugly." In that game the Patriots employed double moves and play action against Polamalu and the top-seeded Steelers, slicing up the league's No. 1 defense in a 41–27 upset win.

Eventually, Polamalu grew comfortable in Dick LeBeau's complex, zone-blitz-heavy 3–4 defense. And LeBeau learned how to employ this distinctive athlete, a 5' 10", 207-pound coil of power with a 43-inch vertical leap.

Deception is vital to any defensive scheme. LeBeau uses Polamalu's versatility to confuse offenses, allowing his safety to line up virtually anywhere on the field as long as Polamalu can perform his assigned task on the play. "He gives us better looks with his instincts than we could ever choreograph," says LeBeau. To illustrate Polamalu's technique, Saints quarterback Drew Brees squatted like a defensive back, statue-still, arms dangling. "This is what he looks like on every play," says Brees. "He doesn't give anything away." Matt Schaub of the Texans said, "What does Polamalu do best? He guesses. He's got confidence that his front seven is going to get pressure on the quarterback, so he's not afraid to attack any area of the field. And he winds up right a lot of the time."

The artist, though, struggles to accept descriptions of his art. "You asked me about the freedom," says Polamalu. "What that really means is that I have more freedom than anybody else to make mistakes. And then my teammates cover them up. You wouldn't believe how many mistakes I make."

Even if that is true, the beauty lies in the chances taken and the moments made. ✦

As a young player Polamalu was often burned when he gambled, but as he matured his risks played out more like sure things.

ANDY RUSSELL

**LINEBACKER 1963, 1966–76
SEVEN-TIME PRO BOWL SELECTION
STEELERS MVP 1971**

A NDY RUSSELL WAS THE FIRST ONE TO the party. A 16th-round draft pick out of Missouri in 1963, he waited a decade for the rest of the Steel Curtain to come together around him. In his first Pro Bowl, in '68, Russell represented a two-win team; in his final two he was joined by seven other Steelers defensive players, all Super Bowl champions. It might as well have been a black-and-gold scrimmage. "I remember one [Pro Bowl] series when all eight of us were on the field," Russell recalled to SI's Paul Zimmerman in '99. "Jack Lambert started calling the defenses. The other three guys said, 'What do we do?' Jack said, 'Just stay out of the way.'" ✦

Russell (34) served in the Army in Germany in 1964 and '65; after returning to the Steelers he became a team captain.

AARON SMITH

DEFENSIVE END 1999–2011
12-YEAR STARTER
2005 PRO BOWL

N 2005 AN OPPOSING SCOUT WAS ASKED TO NAME THE most underrated Steeler, and he chose Aaron Smith. "They don't ask their defensive linemen to make a lot of plays, so you don't see his name much, but he's a big, tough guy who frees up the linebackers," the scout said. Those linebackers may have been the biggest fans of Smith's steadiness and skill. In 2011, Larry Foote told the *Pittsburgh Post-Gazette*, "Never once can I remember leaving the film room saying 'That play was Aaron's fault.' He never was out of position. He never made mistakes." ✦

Smith had totaled 44 career sacks before a foot injury and then neck surgery cut short his 13th season in Pittsburgh.

ERNIE STAUTNER

DEFENSIVE TACKLE/END 1950–1963
PRO FOOTBALL HALL OF FAME 1969
NINE-TIME PRO BOWL SELECTION

FROM LEFT: VIC STEIN/WIREIMAGE.COM; LEIGH WIENER/WIREIMAGE.COM

ERNIE STAUTNER IS THE ONLY STEELER TO have his number officially retired. Though that oddity owes to a change in team policy, it also says something about the respect earned by the smallish (6' 1", 230 pounds) defensive lineman and former U.S. Marine. Stautner played with a doggedness and was impervious to obstacles: When Steelers offensive linemen were injured, he would turn around and play both ways. After retiring he became a defensive coach for the Cowboys, earning two Super Bowl rings—and an excellent location from which to watch the Steelers win two of theirs. ✦

Despite playing on some bad teams, the Bavarian-born Stautner (70) won over fans with his tenaciousness and determination.

DWIGHT WHITE

DEFENSIVE END 1971–1980
TWO-TIME PRO BOWL SELECTION
46 CAREER SACKS

WHITE WAS A VOLUBLE TRASH-TALKER and a Steel Curtain stalwart whose greatest achievement may have been simply showing up. He had been hospitalized with pneumonia the week of Super Bowl IX but rose from his sick bed to play. "I don't know how he did it," Jack Ham told the *Pittsburgh Post-Gazette*. White inspired with his presence and gave the Steelers their first Super Bowl points ever when he downed Fran Tarkenton in the end zone. ✦

The man known as Mad Dog enjoyed his up-close encounters with QBs like the Oilers' Dan Pastorini (right) more than they did.

GEORGE GOJKOVICH/GETTY IMAGES (2)

ROD WOODSON

CORNERBACK 1987–1996
PRO FOOTBALL HALL OF FAME 2009
NFL 75TH ANNIVERSARY TEAM

THE BANNER AT THREE RIVERS DECLARED simply ROD IS GOD, an appropriate sentiment in that Rod Woodson was omnipresent during his 10 seasons with the Steelers. He terrorized offenses as a savage hitter and as a ballhawk— his 71 career interceptions (38 of which came during his years in Pittsburgh) are third most in NFL history. Early on when he returned kicks, he was great at that too. The truest sign of Woodson's rare athletic skills is that he earned All-Pro honors at three positions: cornerback and return man with the Steelers and then safety, the position to which he moved later in his career when he was playing for the Ravens and the Raiders. ✦

Woodson's 17 career TD returns included two on punts, two on kickoffs, one on a fumble and an NFL-record 12 on interceptions.

FROM LEFT: AL TIELEMANS; JOHN BIEVER

THE PRIZE

AL TIELEMANS

When it comes to collecting Super Bowl rings, the Steelers have the proverbial "one for the thumb" and then some

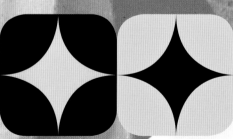

Tackle Marvel Smith enjoyed the taste of victory
after defeating the Seahawks in Super Bowl XL.

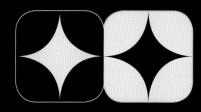

STEELERS 16 ✦ VIKINGS 6

JANUARY 12, 1975   TULANE STADIUM, NEW ORLEANS

How dominant were the Steelers on this day? Game MVP Harris (32) outgained all Vikings rushers by 141 yards.

EXCERPTED FROM SPORTS ILLUSTRATED / JANUARY 20, 1975

The Steelers Sock It To 'Em

BY **DAN JENKINS**

The pile-driving Pittsburgh defense and a grinding ground game gave Minnesota no hope at all, as the Steelers chugged their way to their first title with a decisive 16–6 win on a chilly day in New Orleans

WALTER IOOSS JR.

Greenwood (68) and (left to right)
White, Holmes, Lambert and Ham put
up a solid front against the Vikings.

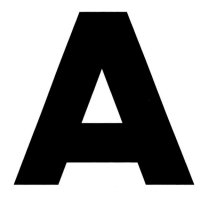

AND NOW, FOR AN ENCORE, the Pittsburgh Steelers' defense will pick up Tulane Stadium and throw it into the middle of Bourbon Street. L.C. Greenwood, or perhaps Mean Joe Greene, will swallow what is left of Fran Tarkenton in a crawfish bisque. Why not? Along with Ernie Holmes and Dwight White, they have already enjoyed dining on the Minnesota running game— has anyone tasted Chuck Foreman's jersey lately?—and making Vikings fly this way and that through the frozen gray sky over New Orleans.

In the 16–6 Super Bowl victory last Sunday that Pittsburgh richly deserved, the Steelers defense was so magnificent that the Viking offense never scored a single point, except two for Pittsburgh. The Steel Curtain was physical and unyielding; at one point, with a yard to go for a first down, Tarkenton decided his best play was a long count that might lure the Steelers offside, evidently because he felt he had no hope of making the yard any other way.

The Steelers defense was so much in control of the game that the Vikings gained only 17 yards on the artificial turf, 12 fewer than Pittsburgh yielded to Oakland in the AFC Championship. Tarkenton must have known it was going to be one of those days. He went to the air early and stayed there, not that it did him much good. Rolling to his right to evade the Pittsburgh defenders who kept swarming after him, he threw 27 times and completed just 11 for only 102 yards. Three of his passes were intercepted, four were deflected and many were hurried.

With defense like this, it was inevitable that the game would have a lot of insane turnaround plays, and it did. How about a safety, which made the score 2–0 Pittsburgh at halftime? Tarkenton, on his own 10-yard line, faked a quick pitchout and tried to hand the ball to Dave Osborn on a dive. But the ball either hit Chuck Foreman's hip or Foreman's hip hit the ball, and the next thing anybody knew Tarkenton was scrambling—after the ball, which was scooting toward the end zone—and being pursued by every Steeler but Art Rooney. Fran prevented a Pittsburgh touchdown by recovering the ball and sliding across the goal line with it for the safety.

Tarkenton was in several other unnatural poses throughout the day because of the Pittsburgh defense. There was the aforementioned occasion when, with fourth-and-one at their 37, the Vikings decided to gamble. They lined up tight. Fran bent over the center and began reciting either the signals or *Swann's Way*. Weeks went by and eventually the play ended up in an argument and no play at all. It was still fourth-and-one and the Vikings decided there was nothing left to do now but punt.

Mullins (72) and the line led the way for Harris; Bradshaw (opposite) directed the final scoring drive in the fourth quarter.

> 'Just hold 'em, we'll get the points,' Andy Russell would say to Terry Bradshaw now and then.

Then there was the time Tarkenton threw two passes on the same play. This was another of those marvelous interludes where Fran was running for life and limb, looking for wide receiver John Gilliam downfield where he might be interfered with—which turned out to be Minnesota's best play all day and, one might add, its only hope. Tarkenton threw the ball. It was deflected by L.C. Greenwood right back to Tarkenton, who threw *another* pass. This one got to Gilliam for an electrifying gain, except that there happens to be this rule that you cannot throw two forward passes on the same play.

In his behalf, it must be noted that Tarkenton did get one drive going toward the end of the first half. He moved Minnesota 55 yards to the Pittsburgh 25. At that point he passed across the middle to Gilliam near the goal line, but the ball was batted out of his hands and Mel Blount intercepted.

The final embarrassment for the Minnesota offense came after it got the biggest break of the game early in the fourth quarter with Pittsburgh leading 9–0. The Steelers' Mike Wagner drew an interference call for shoving Gilliam on a deep pattern, which gave Minnesota a first down at the Pittsburgh five. Suddenly it was a ball game again, but on the first play from scrimmage, Mean Joe Greene pinched so fast on a Foreman stab at the middle that Foreman fumbled, and after poking around for a while Greene came up with the ball. As he trotted off the field, Greene, who earlier had intercepted a pass, gestured triumphantly, shaking his fist at the Vikings, a Steelers way of saying who was the boss. It was the Steelers defense.

In recent weeks, as the Steelers destroyed Buffalo and Oakland on their way to the Super Bowl, the defense had got into the habit of teasing the offense. "Just hold 'em, we'll get the points," linebacker Andy Russell would say to quarterback Terry Bradshaw now and then.

As it happened, Minnesota's defense wasn't bad, either, and it did get the only points the Vikings scored. The touchdown came, typically for this day, on a blocked punt. Matt Blair crashed through to knock down Bobby Walden's punt, the ball bouncing neatly into the hands of Viking Terry Brown in the end zone. But, just as typical of the whole 1974 pro season, Fred Cox saw his placement try for the extra point strike the goalpost and bounce back.

For those who enjoy the mystique of pro football technique, let it now be recorded that the violent Pittsburgh defense was a basic 4–3 with a singular stunt; tackles Joe Greene and Ernie Holmes played over the Minnesota center and crushed him, pinching first one way, then another. The result was that Minnesota's guards could not pull, and thus the Vikings had no blocking for their ground game. Foreman got all their sad handful of rushing yards. Osborn was minus a few. Minnesota coach Bud Grant, having now lost a third Super Bowl, was more bitter than after the other two. He said it was not a good football game. He said, in fact, "There were three bad teams out there. Us, Pittsburgh and the officials."

Greenwood continually harassed Tarkenton (left), who was tackled in the end zone after a fumble for the game's first score.

That was not accurate. Pittsburgh did what it had to do on defense, and in the meantime a couple of guys on the Steelers offense—Bradshaw, the "dumb quarterback," and Franco Harris—did not have at all a bad day. Harris continually tore away at the Vikings, especially in those interludes when Pittsburgh's right guard, Gerry Mullins, was in the process of knocking down Doug Sutherland or Wally Hilgenberg. A fumble on the second-half kickoff gave Pittsburgh the ball at Minnesota's 30, and in four plays the Steelers had a touchdown, largely

CLOCKWISE FROM UPPER RIGHT: HEINZ KLUETMEIER; JAMES DRAKE (2)

FROM LEFT: HEINZ KLUETMEIER; JAMES DRAKE

because of Harris. He rumbled for 24 yards, lost three and then scored from the nine after Mullins got him around the corner with a block on Hilgenberg. Harris scored standing up. He stood up quite a bit on a day when the wind blew at times up to 25 mph and turned a 46° day into a thing where the "chill factor" was 22° for the 80,997 who sat shivering in what was maybe the last game to be played in creaking Tulane Stadium. Harris gained 158 yards in 34 carries to break Larry Csonka's Super Bowl records of 145 and 33. The Steelers gained 249 all told on the ground, with Rocky Bleier running for 65 and Bradshaw adding 33 more.

And it was Terry who saved the day for the Steelers. With the score 9–6 following the blocked punt and more than 10 minutes remaining, plenty of time for the Vikings, who had the wind at their backs, to go ahead and win, Bradshaw took Pittsburgh 66 yards in an 11-play scoring drive that consumed more than seven minutes and ended all real hope for Minnesota. Three times he completed third-down passes, the last a four-yard

Tight end Brown (above) caught the pass that concluded the scoring and sent Steelers coach Chuck Noll (opposite) riding high.

bullet to his tight end, Larry Brown, for a touchdown. In all, Bradshaw hit on nine of 14 for 96 yards.

Bradshaw said afterward, "I've looked at all sides—being a hero and being a jerk. I think I can handle this very well." Something will probably be made of the fact that Bradshaw changed his shoes at halftime, slipping into a pair that had longer cleats, the better to stand up, drop back, roll out or bootleg on the fake turf. (Slippery spots, caused, some claimed, by pockets of air and water beneath the surface, had Steelers slipping repeatedly.) Yet all that needs to be said of Bradshaw is that he has risen to the challenge of his team's three playoff games—against the Bills, Raiders and Vikings—and left each as the best quarterback on the field and, not incidentally, the winning one. ✦

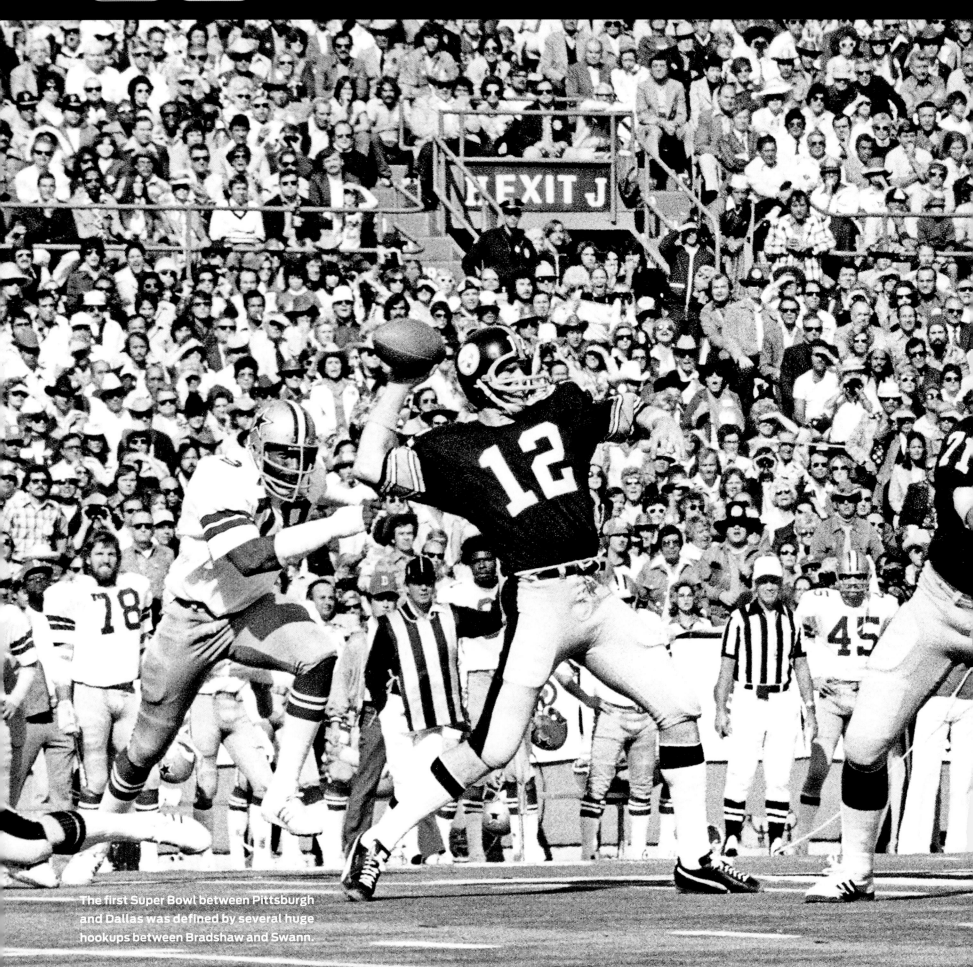

The first Super Bowl between Pittsburgh and Dallas was defined by several huge hookups between Bradshaw and Swann.

SUPER BOWL

NFLWIREIMAGE.COM

EXCERPTED FROM SPORTS ILLUSTRATED / JANUARY 26, 1976

Dallas Feels the Steeler Crunch

BY **DAN JENKINS**

There was drama aplenty in Pittsburgh's 21–17 takedown of the Cowboys, but the day belonged to Lynn Swann, who delivered a crucial score and also one of the great highlights in Super Bowl history

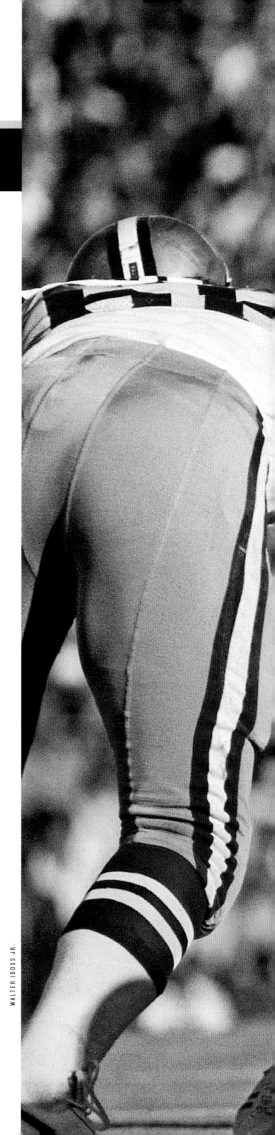

WALTER IOOSS JR.

The Pittsburgh defense intimidated Dallas all day, with the line sacking Staubach seven times and Lambert (58) memorably tossing a Cowboy to the ground in response to a perceived taunt.

FOR ALL OF THOSE GAUDY THINGS that happened throughout the afternoon, memories of the 1976 Super Bowl will keep going back to the Pittsburgh Steelers' Lynn Swann climbing into the air like the boy in the Indian rope trick, and coming down with the football. He didn't come down with very many passes last Sunday, really, only four, but he caught the ones that truly mattered. That is why it will seem that he spent the day way up there in the crisp sky, a thousand feet above Miami's Orange Bowl, where neither the Dallas Cowboys nor even a squadron of fighter planes could do anything to stop him. When it was all over Lynn Swann and the Steelers had won 21–17 and had repeated as the champions of professional madness.

The thinking beforehand was that Pittsburgh could win this game only if Franco Harris trampled over and through a thing called the flex defense of the intellectual Cowboys who, in the meantime, on offense, would do enough weird things to the hard-hat Steelers to capture the day and write a perfect finish to their storybook season. Essentially Dallas stopped Harris, however, and the winning of Super Bowl X was left up to Swann and the indomitable Terry Bradshaw, who seems to collect concussions and championship rings with equal facility. Just for good measure there also was a defense that could probably take apart an attacking tank battalion if it had to. But mainly it was Swann, who in the fourth quarter would make the biggest catch of the day, a 64-yard touchdown heave from Bradshaw, who didn't realize until much later, after his head stopped rattling, that he had passed for a touchdown. This was the play that put the Steelers safely ahead 21–10. Only a few impossible last-minute deeds by the Cowboys could have changed the outcome of Super Bowl

From any angle Swann's soaring 53-yard catch was remarkable for its virtuosity, though it would lead only to a failed field goal attempt; of his 64-yard touchdown grab in the fourth quarter he would say modestly, "All I did was run under the ball."

X, and they just were not quite a good enough football team to pull it off.

That last catch of Swann's has to be dwelled on, for it had Super Bowl trophy and $15,000 to each Steeler written all over it. The play ended with Swann catching a rocket from Bradshaw that traveled at least 70 yards in the air, Swann jumping and taking it on the Dallas five-yard line and gliding in for the touchdown, and Bradshaw barely conscious on the ground after being decked by Cliff Harris on a safety blitz. Players who are involved in such heroics seldom have much to say afterwards that would give them more meaning. Swann said, "All I did was run under the ball." He thought for a moment and figured there must be more to it than that. He remembered that earlier, referring to another pass, Cliff Harris had told him, "You're lucky you didn't come back on that ball because I'm gonna take a shot at you. You better watch your head."

There were enough bizarre events throughout the game to daze the most ardent fan. Dallas took a 7–0 lead, the touchdown resulting from a blunder on the part of Bobby Walden, the Steelers' punter. He had a good snap from center and he simply dropped it. The Cowboys' rush blanketed him and it was Dallas's ball at the Steeler 29. In one play the Cowboys scored, as Drew Pearson ran a crossing pattern over the middle and was wide-open. Roger Staubach laid the ball in beautifully and it was six points. The Steelers' safety, Mike Wagner, who claimed the fault was his because he misread the play, would have his revenge later.

Pittsburgh tied it up 7–7, with Bradshaw starting on his 33 and giving the ball to Harris and Rocky Bleier, who nibbled away to the Dallas 48. Then came a 32-yard pass to Swann down the right sideline, on which he made his first award-winning catch of the day, setting up a scoring pass to tight end Randy Grossman.

Dallas came back with a field goal by Toni Fritsch to go into the lead 10–7. It could have been 10–10 at the half, but Pittsburgh's Roy Gerela missed a field goal that wasted Swann's next sensational performance, a tumbling, juggling catch of a 53-yard Bradshaw bomb.

It was not until the fourth quarter that either team scored again. This time it was two points for Pittsburgh as Reggie Harrison flashed in to block Mitch Hoopes's punt for a safety. Dallas 10, Pittsburgh 9. The Steelers finally went ahead when Gerela, who by then had missed another field goal, knocked one through from the 26-yard line.

So it was a 12–10 game, with less than half of the final quarter left, when Wagner got his revenge. Staubach dropped back from his 15 to try the same type of pass Pearson had caught for the touchdown. Wagner reacted as if he and Staubach had concocted the play together. He lurked just out of

Gerela missed two field goals and an extra point attempt but hit on kicks from 36 and 18 yards in the fourth quarter.

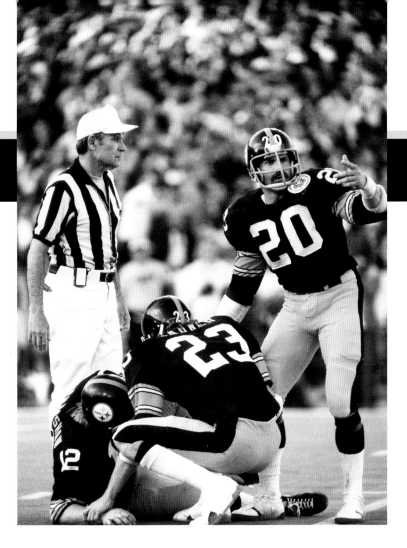

Bradshaw threw for 209 yards on only nine completions, including two passes to John Stallworth (opposite), but after being bulldozed on his final throw, the TD to Swann, he was helped off the field and watched the rest of the game from the sideline.

Pearson's sight, and when the ball arrived Wagner picked it off and went screaming down to the Dallas seven. To the credit of the Dallas defense, it held the Steelers to Gerela's second field goal. Next came Swann's dramatic touchdown catch to make it 21–10, followed by a Staubach to Percy Howard pass of 34 yards, which concluded the scoring at 21–17.

As for all that mischief in the waning moments of the game, it started when the Steelers decided to use up time by running on fourth down instead of punting. But the clock stopped when Dallas took over near midfield, leaving 1:22 to play and giving Staubach and Drew Pearson an excellent chance to produce their old miracle. The Steelers' weird decision may best be explained by a little scene that was taking place in a booth upstairs. A frantic Pittsburgh assistant coach began hollering at Art McNally, the NFL's Supervisor of Officials. From the opposite side of a plexiglass divider covered with brown paper he shouted something on the order of, "The clock stopped, McNally! Hey, McNally, they're not running the clock!"

To which McNally calmly replied, "The clock always stops when the ball changes hands." Evidently the Steelers brain trust was so pleased that Dallas had used up all of its timeouts on defense that they had forgotten the rule, and now they could only be aghast at their folly. Only when Staubach's final throw was intercepted in the end zone was the win secure.

Even without the excitement on the field, there were enough trappings to make the game memorable—for one thing, it was surely the first time a press box ever had Raquel Welch hanging around in it. But the Cowboys, apparently determined to start things off with a flair, had the audacity to run a reverse on the opening kickoff. Preston Pearson handed the ball off to Tom Henderson, an ebullient special-team rookie, and after Henderson had galloped 48 yards right past the Steelers' bench, everyone knew this was going to break the mold of those Super Bowls of the past.

Dallas started right off doing things that enraged the Steelers' emotional leader, middle linebacker Jack Lambert. "They mess up your head too much," Lambert had said before the game. "If they beat you, you feel like you've been tricked instead of whipped. I hate teams like that."

For most of the afternoon Lambert looked as if he hated everybody in white. The Steelers didn't draw a penalty the entire game, but it was not because Lambert didn't try, particularly on one very visible occasion. Gerela had missed a field goal in the second quarter and Dallas's Cliff Harris was so pleased that he slapped Lambert on the helmet and then said thank you to Gerela. No one could tell whether it was a playful pat on Lambert's helmet, but they did see Lambert grab Harris and throw him down.

Referee Norm Schachter stepped in and began moving Lambert backwards, warning him that he had better cool off. "I smiled," Lambert said, thereby revealing a facet of his character hitherto well masked.

It was somewhat in character for the Cowboys not to realize what a spectacle the game had been. They reacted to the loss with a humor and graciousness that reflects Landry's control of the squad.

"Was it exciting?" Dallas tight end Jean Fugett said. "I guess it was. I guess maybe we can't play a dull game."

Neither can Lynn Swann. And the combination of Dallas being there and Swann rising to the occasion—up, up and away—made it something for everybody in Miami to take home to think about until next year. Who said the Super Bowl is dull? ✦

STEELERS 35 ✦ COWBOYS 31

JANUARY 21, 1979 ORANGE BOWL, MIAMI

An interception by Mel Blount (47) was one of three turnovers forced by the Pittsburgh defense.

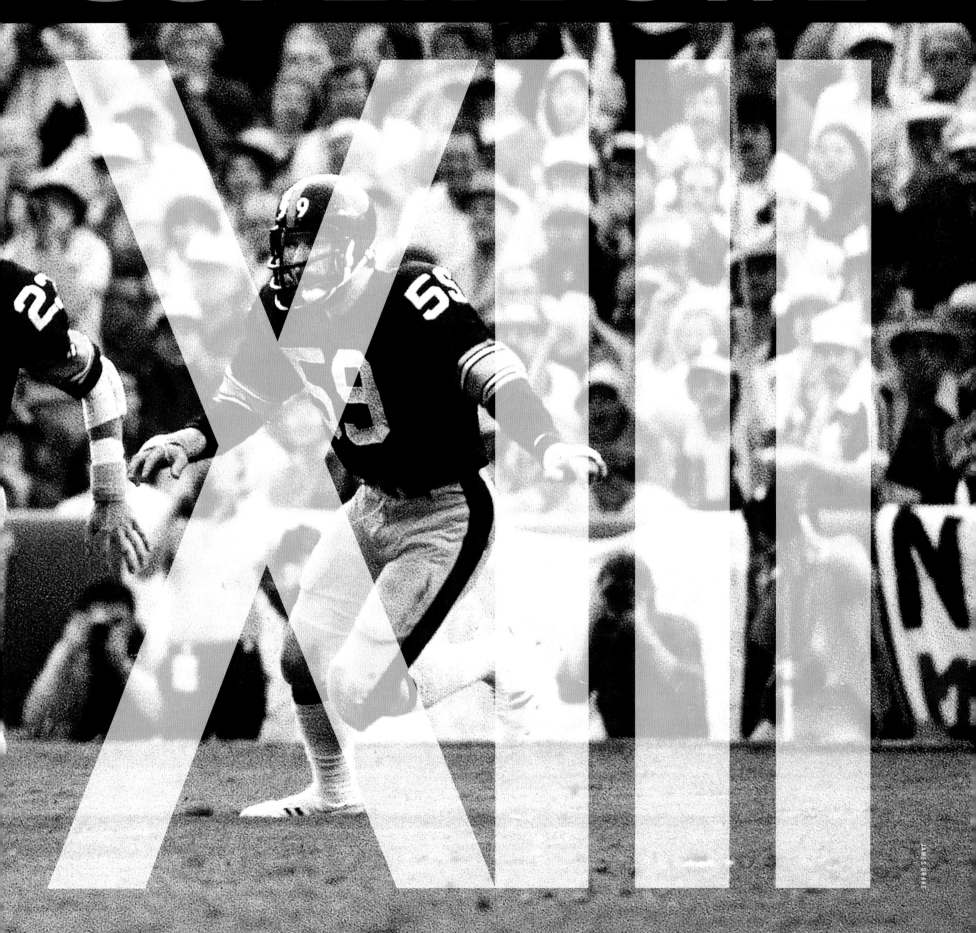

SUPER BOWL

XIII

EXCERPTED FROM SPORTS ILLUSTRATED / JANUARY 29, 1979

What a Passing Parade It Was!

BY **DAN JENKINS**

When the Steelers beat the Cowboys the second time around, it was Terry Bradshaw who took control, throwing for the most yards and touchdowns in the young history of the Super Bowl

WALTER IOOSS JR.

Bradshaw's bounty for the day included 318 passing yards, four touchdowns, his third Super Bowl ring and his first MVP trophy.

FOR THREE QUARTERS AND ALMOST SIX minutes of the fourth last Sunday, Super Bowl XIII, which Pittsburgh wound up winning 35–31, was everything professional football's championship game is supposed to be, but rarely is. It had the NFL's two best teams, the Pittsburgh Steelers and the Dallas Cowboys, doing amazing things in heroic—and sometimes haphazard, even peculiar—fashion on the damp Orange Bowl turf.

It had Tony Dorsett scuttling around and through the Steelers on the game's first drive only to have the Cowboys fumble away the ball on an ill-conceived, triple handoff gadget play that was supposed to end with a pass thrown by quarterback Roger Staubach.

It had Terry Bradshaw passing the Steelers to a quick 7–0 lead on a 28-yard lob to John Stallworth in the end zone at the end of a bang-bang 53-yard drive. It had Bradshaw losing the ball on a fumble, and then three plays later Staubach combining with Tony Hill on a 39-yard touchdown pass play that tied the score at 7–7 on the last play of the first quarter. It had Bradshaw, after recovering his own fumble in the backfield, being sandwiched by linebackers Thomas (Hollywood) Henderson and Mike Hegman, with Henderson pinning Bradshaw's arms while Hegman pickpocketed the ball and ran 37 yards for a touchdown and a 14–7 Dallas lead. It had Bradshaw complaining that his left shoulder was sore and being told by a team doctor that it might be separated.

It had Bradshaw immediately returning to the game and throwing a short first-down pass to the ubiquitous Stallworth, who turned it into a 75-yard touchdown play as Dallas cornerback Aaron Kyle, who had been burned on the first touchdown, missed a tackle. It had Bradshaw sending Pittsburgh to the locker room with a 21–14 halftime lead by lofting a seven-yard pass to a leaping Rocky Bleier in the end zone.

Then, in the third quarter, it had Dallas, suddenly starting to look like the better team, all set to tie the score at 21–21, only to have tight end Jackie Smith—with nary a Steeler in sight—drop Staubach's eminently catchable pass in the end zone. The Cowboys had to settle for Rafael Septien's 27-yard field goal.

And now, six minutes into the fourth quarter, the Steelers were desperately clinging to a 21–17 lead—the same score, incidentally, by which they had defeated the Cowboys in Super Bowl X in Miami—and Bradshaw was dropping back and, under pressure, hoisting the football into one of Lynn Swann's holding patterns 33 yards downfield. Swann and Dallas cornerback Benny Barnes were chasing the ball in relatively close file, with Barnes slightly in the lead, when Barnes slipped or tripped or stumbled and fell. Swann tripped over Barnes and fell, stretching out vainly for Bradshaw's pass at the Dallas 23-yard line.

Field judge Fred Swearingen threw his yellow flag. To those who saw it live, the pass play looked to be a case of two players bumping and tripping over each other.

Tight end Randy Grossman (left) caught three balls for 29 yards, while Bleier's one reception was a seven-yard score late in the second quarter.

That is the way Swearingen apparently saw it, too, but his flag meant one of two things: *offensive* pass interference on Swann for tripping Barnes, or *defensive* pass interference on Barnes for tripping Swann.

The call was against Barnes, and Pittsburgh had a first down. Four plays later Franco Harris crashed up the middle on a 22-yard trap play to put the Steelers ahead 28–17, and there were only seven minutes to go. If that turn of events demoralized the Cowboys, what happened on the ensuing kickoff shattered them.

Dallas inexplicably stationed defensive tackle Randy White, who was playing with a cast on his fractured left thumb, in the middle of the field near the 25-yard line as Roy Gerela prepared to kick off. Pittsburgh coach Chuck Noll had called Gerela to the sideline for a brief conference following Gerela's successful conversion, and told him to kick deep. But Gerela slipped and his kick bounced directly to the 250-pound White, who had no clear idea what to do with it. He half fumbled and half lateraled the ball, only to have it wind up in the hands of Pittsburgh's Dennis (Dirt) Winston at the Dallas 18.

Before Tom Landry could even grimace, Bradshaw—who enjoyed his most productive day as a pro, throwing for 318 yards and four touchdowns, both Super Bowl records—fired a first-down pass into the end zone that Swann leaped high and plucked from out of the night, as only he can. And the riskiest Super Bowl of them all was a rout, with the Steelers leading 35–17. The elapsed time between the two touchdowns was 19 seconds.

Staubach then rallied the Cowboys against Pittsburgh's obviously relaxed defense. He threw a seven-yard touchdown pass to Billy Joe DuPree at the end of an 89-yard drive, which was highlighted by Tony Dorsett's 29-yard run. After Dallas recovered an onside kick, Staubach passed four yards for a touchdown to a wide-open Butch Johnson. With the score now 35–31 and 22 seconds to play, Dallas would have one last chance if it recovered another onside kick. But Septien kicked the ball squarely to Bleier, who fell on it at the Dallas 45, and a disgruntled Bradshaw ran out the clock.

"Our guys started celebrating when it was 35–17," Bradshaw said later, "and it made me mad. They were slapping hands and shaking hands and saying how great it was. But it wasn't so great, because the game wasn't over."

Besides Bradshaw's arm and his superb receivers (Stallworth, who did not play in the second half because of a muscle cramp, caught three passes for 115 yards and his two touchdowns: Swann caught seven for 124 yards and his score), the other thing that helped defeat the Cowboys was the touchdown they blew late in the third quarter, which would have tied the score at 21–21. Smith, the marvelous old former St. Louis Cardinal whom Dallas had called out of retirement in September, flat-out dropped Staubach's pass in the end zone.

Stallworth snagged three balls for 115 yards and two touchdowns, part of a glorious day for the Pittsburgh pass catchers (above).

The play came from Landry, and it was an inspired call. The ball was on the Pittsburgh 10, third-and-three. Landry sent in an extra tight end, Smith, indicating a run. Dallas lined up with Scott Laidlaw as a single setback and Dorsett went in motion to his right. But instead of handing off to Laidlaw or passing in the flat to Dorsett, the most likely eventualities, Staubach threw over the middle to the 38-year-old Smith who was wide-open. However, the ball was low and slightly behind Smith. Staubach says he threw it too softly, and that that's why Smith, who was on his knees, dropped it.

"He was so open I could have punted it to him," said Staubach sorrowfully.

Smith could only say, "It was a beautiful play that coach Landry conceived. When I slipped, I guess I was just trying to be overcautious, and that's why I dropped it."

For Pittsburgh, nobody dropped anything that mattered. Stallworth's two touchdown pass plays were very different, and they both say something about Bradshaw. The first was a cunning 28-yard beauty—the Steelers call it "One Eleven Out"—that Bradshaw thought would take advantage of Kyle on Stallworth, man-for-man, and it did. Stallworth got behind Kyle and caught the ball easily in the end zone.

The second came at what might be described as a mildly opportune time: in the second quarter, after the Cowboys had taken their 14–7 lead by virtue of the Brink's Job that Henderson and Hegman had performed

on Bradshaw. Bad shoulder or no bad shoulder, Bradshaw was right back running for his life again. This time he found Stallworth at the Pittsburgh 35. Stallworth shook off a glancing blow by Kyle—more or less a flesh wound—and outran everybody for the score.

Earlier, in what was as wildly exciting a first half as two good teams have ever played, in or out of the Super Bowl, the Cowboys had done something no other club had achieved against the Steelers all season. They scored a touchdown in the first quarter.

Granted, it was on the last play, when Staubach connected with Hill, but Dallas already had hinted very strongly that it could move the football and, surprisingly, that it could move it on the ground, most notably with Dorsett, who gained a tough 96 yards on 15 carries running traps and misdirected sweeps.

All game long, though, it was Bradshaw who was the dominant presence. "Today I relaxed, felt good and had fun," said Bradshaw, who was the unanimous choice for MVP. "I had a little bit of a lackadaisical attitude. I didn't want to get uptight. I don't need anyone telling me how great or how smart I am, or how smart I'm not, I just tried to go out there and help win a football game."

Which he did—and how. ✦

After Smith's third-quarter drop of a touchdown (left), Harris (below) scored and Pittsburgh rolled to title number 3.

Harris scored two touchdowns, both on one-yard runs, this one coming early in the second quarter.

EXCERPTED FROM SPORTS ILLUSTRATED / JANUARY 28, 1980

They Were Just Too Much

BY **PAUL ZIMMERMAN**

The Rams and their young quarterback Vince Ferragamo gave the Steelers a tougher fight than anticipated, but in the end the Steel Curtain—era greats came through to claim their final ring

WALTER IOOSS JR.

Greene realized that a win over the Rams and a fourth Super Bowl title in six years would lift the Steelers to historic status.

PETER READ MILLER

T WAS AN EMOTIONAL SUPER BOWL AND EASILY THE best of the XIV played so far. It was the way Super Bowls are supposed to be played, but haven't been. The lead changed hands six times before it ended Pittsburgh 31, Los Angeles 19, but only the guys who laid the 11 points with the bookies read it as a 12-point Steeler win. The Rams made it that close. They stayed in it because of a sustained intensity that brought them great honor, because of an unexpectedly brilliant performance by young quarterback Vince Ferragamo, and because of a tackle-to-tackle ferocity that had the Steelers defense on its heels much of the afternoon.

But the Steelers aren't exactly virgins in this type of warfare, and when they needed the great plays they got them. The Steelers routinely make the great plays, and when you get all excited about those feats, they'll look at you level and say things like: "I've made better catches in Super Bowls . . . a couple of one-handers one time" (John Stallworth); or "It's part of our basic coverage . . . it's on the films" (Jack Lambert); or "I really didn't think it would work . . . I hadn't been completing it in practice" (Terry Bradshaw).

Which is why the Steelers have won four Super Bowl rings in the last six years, and why Joe Greene can say, "This game was an invitation engraved in gold."

"An invitation to what?" someone asked, on cue.

"To immortality . . . along with those tremendous pacesetters, the Green Bay Packers," Greene said. He thought for a moment and then added, "Next year it'll all be forgotten. It'll be, 'What have you done for me lately?' A vicious, vicious cycle."

As the Steelers discovered on Sunday, it's getting tougher and tougher to stay on top. Two weeks before, Houston was supposed to roll over—but hadn't; the Oilers had hung tough until the fourth quarter of the AFC Championship Game. This time it was the Rams who were supposed to lie down. The betting was even money that Ferragamo, making only his eighth start, would not be in at the end. The only Ferragamo interview of note that had appeared in the papers during the week was a piece about his malapropisms: "How they arrived at their conclusions behooves me," etc.

But Ferragamo was clear-headed in Pasadena, and he led a very spirited team. As the clubs changed ends to start the fourth quarter with the Rams leading 19–17, a significant thing happened. The Rams had intercepted Bradshaw—for the third time—at the L.A. four-yard line, and Wendell Tyler had broken one for 13 yards, out to the 17, behind a big block by his fullback, Cullen Bryant. Then the whistle blew, and next thing you knew, the Rams were sprinting for the other end of the field.

"We talked about doing it," said left tackle Doug France. "It was a very good psych; it let them know we were ready to go. We had 83 yards to cover, and we had to show them we had the strength to do it. We were saying to them, 'Hey, we're not that tired.'"

The Steelers took their time switching ends. No sense getting all excited about a change of quarters.

"No, I didn't see it," Greene said of the L.A. sprint. "I had other things on my mind."

Lambert (58) planned to gang-tackle Tyler (26) and force fumbles, but the Rams back showed unexpected mettle, holding on to the ball all day.

> "'Lambert hollered so loud in the huddle that I got scared,' said Shell. 'I can't repeat what he said.'"

Swann (88) had five catches for 79 yards and this third-quarter touchdown but was forced to leave the game after a hard hit.

"I think the Rams were just excited," said cornerback Mel Blount, like Greene a veteran of Steeler coach Chuck Noll's eight playoff teams. "You know, it's the Super Bowl and all that."

If Hollywood, not Pasadena, had been hosting XIV, the Rams would have driven those 83 yards and put the game away, and the losingest team—9–7 on the regular season—ever to come into a Super Bowl would have tasted the golden bubbly. But what happened was that the Rams ran three plays, gained six yards and had to punt. And it was a terrific punt by Ken Clark, 59 yards, one yard short of his career best. The Steelers got the ball on their own 25, and, hey, the Rams were still on top of this game.

First-and-10: Jack Reynolds stuffs Franco Harris after a couple of yards. Second-and-eight: Sidney Thornton drops a screen pass, but the play is messed up anyway because Gerry Mullins, the Steeler right guard, is 10 yards downfield. Hang on, Rams, the champs are coming apart. Third-and-eight at the Pittsburgh 27 and what to do? Normally, the Steelers would have gone into a three-wide-receiver set and tried to work something underneath for the first down, but they didn't have three wide receivers left.

Lynn Swann had given the Steelers a brief 17–13 lead in the third quarter with a leaping catch of a 47-yard touchdown pass, but he had been knocked out of the game one series later as the result of a very bad decision by Bradshaw. Bradshaw had rolled to his left, looking for help, and had dumped the ball to Swann, curling to the left side. Throw late over the middle and you run the risk of getting either an interception or one of your receivers killed. Bradshaw got the ball high to Swann, who got a very rough ride from cornerback Pat Thomas. When Swann came to, his vision was blurred and one whole area was totally blank. "Lower right quadrant," he said. "I couldn't see anything at all in that area. The doc told me I'd had it for the day."

Theo Bell, a backup receiver for the Steelers, had been removed from the game after taking a vicious shot by linebacker George Andrews on a punt, and now, with third-and-eight on their own 27, with a little over 12 minutes to go and trailing by two points, the Steelers had only two wide receivers left on the roster. Bennie Cunningham, the tight end, split wide left. Jim Smith, Swann's backup, was wide right, and Stallworth was in the slot inside him. Chuck Noll sent in the play: "60 Prevent Slot Hook and Go." A pass to Stallworth, who would make a little hitch inside and then take off.

"I didn't like the call," Bradshaw said. "I hadn't been hitting that pass all week. It's a matter of building confidence. You don't build confidence in things that don't work. Maybe it was our ace in the hole, I don't know."

It hadn't been a good week for Bradshaw. He was beat, having slept only four or five hours a night. The night before the game he went to bed at midnight but woke up at 3 a.m. "I couldn't get back to sleep," he said. He had dragged through the practices, the interview sessions, the pre–Super Bowl madness that turned the Steelers' Newport Beach hotel into a zoo. Meanwhile, the Rams were practicing on their home turf over in Anaheim and going home to the wife and kiddies. On Thursday, Bradshaw gave one of his zillion radio interviews of the week. His answers were mechanical.

"You certainly seem laid-back going into this game," the guy with the mike said.

"Yeah, well, you know, we've been here before," Bradshaw said, giving stock answer No. 435.

"Laid-back, hell, I'm tired. Tired," he said later. "I'm not sleeping. I just can't sleep. . . . I don't know what it is. Pressure, I guess. Tension. I've never felt it this bad. I haven't thrown the ball well in two weeks. I'm just tired of football. Drained."

Ray Mansfield, the old Steeler center, dropped by the hotel to visit with his former teammates. "I could always look at Terry before a game and tell you what kind of a day he was going to have," Mansfield said. "If he was a little glassy-eyed, I'd know it was going to be a long afternoon."

"How does he look today?" Mansfield was asked.

"Don't ask," he said.

And now the coach is telling Bradshaw that his arm is going to win it. Bradshaw's first interception, which had set up a Rams' go-ahead field goal—13–10—in the second quarter, had brought back visions of the interception Houston's Vernon Perry ran back for a TD in the AFC title game. His first interception against the Rams had been a late throw over the middle to Swann; Bradshaw had tried to force the ball through double coverage, and Dave Elmendorf had picked it off. Bradshaw's second interception had been a ball that got away from him, a bloop throw to Smith on a deep pattern. His third one had been a force to Stallworth over the middle, deep in Ram territory, with the Steelers behind 19–17.

There had almost been a fourth one. In the third quarter, with the Rams still on top 19–17, Bradshaw had tried to find Swann inside, and Nolan Cromwell, the L.A. free safety, had roared up like the Duesenberg that had transported Steeler patriarch Art Rooney out for the coin toss. "The only thing that could have stopped him," said Steeler center Mike Webster, "was a .357 Magnum." But Cromwell dropped the ball.

Third-and-eight on the 27. Your game to win, Terry baby. The Steelers'

Three future Hall of Famers had to bide their time on the sideline in a game in which the lead changed hands six times.

running game? Forget it. Thirty-seven carries for only 84 yards on the day. "The Rams did their homework," Webster said. "When we'd audible, Jack Reynolds would call the correct defense for the play we audibled to. They knew us."

"I could see them doing research on the sidelines," Rams defensive end Fred Dryer said. "I think Terry was having trouble reading us."

There are not many ways a human being can throw a football better than Bradshaw did to Stallworth on that third-and-eight play. Stallworth got inside Rod Perry, the cornerback, and behind Elmendorf, the strong safety, and took it 73 yards for a 24–19 Pittsburgh lead. Two series later Stallworth did it again—45 yards on the same play— only this time he didn't bother to throw the little inside fake. It set

> **'The real fact,' Greene said, 'was that we just had too many good football players.'**

up Franco Harris's one-yard touchdown for the 31–19 margin that rewarded the Steelers bettors.

"God-given ability," Webster said. "You just can't beat it. Terry had enough ability to overcome the mistakes, the three interceptions, the bad week he'd had. He had the courage to go with that long stuff."

In the Rams' locker room Perry answered the same question over and over: "Inside-outside coverage. I had the outside. I did the best I could. Hey, haven't you ever seen a perfect play?"

Emotions were running high in that dressing room. On his way in, Tyler had turned to the writers and said, "I didn't fumble in the game. Put that in your paper!" Tyler never fumbled. No one did. The Steelers banged Tyler around plenty too. Knocked him out of the game five times. Count 'em. But he kept coming back.

"We wanted to gang-tackle him because he has a reputation for fumbling," Lambert said. "We wanted to make him know he'd been in a football game."

It went both ways. On his third carry Tyler broke a 39-yarder, which set up the Rams' first score and gave them a 7–3 lead. Faked two guys off their feet on the slippery sideline turf.

"It set the tone," Greene said. "Put us in the tank, so to speak."

In a corner Ferragamo was trying to describe what it had been like to face 103,985 fans and 11 Steelers in his first Super Bowl. "I tried audibling one

Stallworth's 73-yard touchdown catch (left) provided reason to celebrate as the Steelers finally reclaimed the lead for good.

FROM LEFT: WALTER IOOSS JR.; HEINZ KLUETMEIER

time at the noisy end of the field," he said. "No one heard me. I was a little leery about audibling after that. There was a 30-second clock, but it was kind of concealed. It was tough to see until it started getting dark. It was there for you, though, if you could make it out. Hell, you'd better make it out."

Ferragamo was asked a technical question. "I tried zooming—and motion—they took me out of it," he said. No one knew what he was talking about. Ferragamo stopped for a moment and looked up. "It just hurts to know you're that good and you can't win it," he said. "It's a hurting feeling inside."

It was a strange role-reversal for the clubs. The Rams were the muscle team, not the Steelers. L.A. established a running game very early and worked it. The Steelers went big play, big gamble. Three big plays, three interceptions.

"Anyone who calls us dogs," Jack Youngblood, the Rams' defensive end, said, "well, let him call me that to my face."

"We gave it everything we had, we went out there with everything in our hearts," Dennis Harrah, the L.A. right guard, was saying. "We picked up all their stunts, all their defensive-line games. I think we surprised them with our guts and determination."

He was looking at the floor. When he looked up, you could see he was crying. "I'm sorry, but I just can't talk about it anymore," Harrah said.

Jim Jodat, a reserve running back, put his arm around Harrah. "C'mon, man, the bus is leaving," he said.

"I'll be all right," Harrah said.

There were times when the Pittsburgh defense looked shaky, when it looked as if the Steelers were barely hanging on. They reached Ferragamo for four sacks, but they had to use multiple blitzes to do it. Ferragamo said, "On one of them—when we were down on their 13 and they put 11 men up on the line and sacked me—well, maybe I should have called timeout before I ran the play. Maybe it's inexperience. We'll be back here again."

The Rams fooled the Steelers secondary on their last touchdown, a 24-yard halfback option pass, Lawrence McCutcheon to Ron Smith, that gave them the 19–17 lead. L.A. did a number on Ron Johnson, the left corner, on that play. Johnson had been having words with Billy Waddy, the Rams' wide receiver. Then Waddy, on an underthrown ball, had caught a 50-yarder on Johnson, the kind of catch that drives cornerbacks crazy. The book says you don't let crazy cornerbacks off the hook, so the Rams swept McCutcheon to Johnson's side, and when Johnson was drawn into the net, it was time for McCutcheon to stand and deliver to Smith. Six points.

"You could see we were getting to them," said Gordon Gravelle, the reserve L.A. tackle who used to be a Steeler. "At times they looked a little confused out there. I haven't seen that on a Pittsburgh team in a long while."

"Jack Lambert hollered so hard in the huddle in the first half that I got scared," said Steelers safety Donnie Shell. "I can't repeat what he said, but he got real red in the face. He said we were sleepwalking out there."

The final chapter is that the Steelers' big-play people—the guys who had done it so many times before—rose up one more time.

"The real fact," Greene said, "was that we just had too many good football players."

He looked at his audience. "You can't beat talent," he said. ✦

SUPER BOWL XL

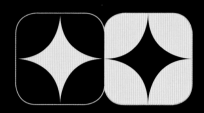

STEELERS 21 ✦ SEAHAWKS 10

FEBRUARY 5, 2006   FORD FIELD, DETROIT

The win over Seattle featured several close officiating calls, including Roethlisberger's keeper that was ruled a touchdown.

EXCERPTED FROM SPORTS ILLUSTRATED / FEBRUARY 13, 2006

Steelers Ride High in Motown

BY **MICHAEL SILVER**

Twenty-six Super Bowls had to roll on by before Pittsburgh could finally claim that one for the thumb, and they did so by soundly defeating the Seahawks 21–10 behind an MVP performance by Hines Ward

BOB ROSATO

Ward caught five passes for 123 yards, including this fourth-quarter touchdown that gave the Steelers an 11-point lead and left the future *Dancing with the Stars* contestant jumping for joy.

THE HIT CAUGHT HINES WARD OFF-guard, momentarily jolting the Steelers' inexorable wideout. Craning his neck to see who was wrapping him up from behind, Ward eyeballed a laughing man with long hair, dark sunglasses and a weathered cowboy hat. The receiver smiled broadly at one of the Steelers' most famous fans, singer Hank Williams Jr., who had joined hundreds of revelers at the Pontiac Marriott in suburban Detroit in the early hours of Monday morning. "Remember when I saw you in training camp and you were calling me Mr. Hank?" asked Williams, a frequent visitor to the team's headquarters. "Well, you're Mr. Hines today. In fact, you're the entertainer of the year."

Several hours earlier Ward had regaled a Pittsburgh-heavy crowd of 68,206 at Ford Field, and a worldwide television audience, with his distinctive, proletarian brand of football, blocking, catching passes and ramrodding his way to MVP honors in the Steelers' 21–10 victory over the Seattle Seahawks in Super Bowl XL. Later on Monday he would fly to Disney World with teammate Jerome Bettis, who announced his retirement after the game, then zoom back to Pittsburgh for a victory parade through the city's streets on Tuesday. But Ward is one player who is sure to stay grounded in the face of his burgeoning fame.

A former college quarterback and tailback at Georgia who fought his way to All-Pro status despite having lost his left anterior cruciate ligament in childhood, Ward is the NFL's anti-Terrell Owens: a selfless star revered by his coaches and fellow Steelers. "Hines's character symbolizes what kind of team this is: close-knit and physical," outside linebacker Clark Haggans said in Pittsburgh's jubilant locker room after the franchise had won its NFL-record-tying fifth Super Bowl title. "He's the best receiver in football and one of the toughest people I've ever been around."

Are you ready for some football, Steelers style? The Seahawks weren't, spoiling the first Super Bowl appearance in franchise history by making more mistakes and fewer big plays than a Pittsburgh team that appeared more vulnerable than a Detroit autoworker. Despite a shaky performance from second-year quarterback Ben Roethlisberger and the virtual disappearance of their two marquee defenders, wild-haired strong safety Troy Polamalu and outspoken outside linebacker Joey Porter, the Steelers plodded to victory in a game that will be remembered less for the caliber of play than for what its outcome represented: one for the thumb, finally, for 73-year-old Pittsburgh owner Dan Rooney, whose club won four Super Bowls in the 1970s; a crowning career achievement for coach Bill Cowher, in his 14th season with the Steelers; and a confirmation that faith in one another and accountability can carry a team past seemingly insurmountable odds.

Bettis turned into a blocking back for Roethlisberger on the one-yard touchdown run that gave the Steelers their first score and a 7–3 lead.

SUPER BOWL XL

'I was so excited,' Randle El said later of the trick play, 'I had to make sure I didn't give it away.'

Cowher pushed the right buttons on a surprisingly sloppy Super Sunday, but his most important move might have come two months earlier, when he walked into a meeting room at the Steelers' training facility the morning after a 38–31 home loss to the Cincinnati Bengals. That setback had essentially ceded the AFC North title to the Bengals and put Pittsburgh, at 7–5, on the brink of playoff elimination. The players shuddered. Would Cowher launch a spit-filled tirade? Would his head explode?

To the Steelers' relief, the man with football's most celebrated chin turned junior high history teacher instead. Passing out grade sheets, Cowher gave his players an assignment: Watch film of the Cincinnati game and for every play assign yourself a grade (plus or minus) in each of three categories: technique, effort and how well you followed your assignment. "It was revealing," Cowher recalled last Thursday morning in the cafeteria area of the team's hotel in Pontiac. "Some guys, like Troy, were overly critical of themselves; others were a little too lenient. But the most important point I wanted to make was that if each guy did just a little bit more and was accountable for his actions, we could turn this thing around—together." Said Bettis, the 33-year-old running back, "It drove home the message: Before you start to point fingers, you've got to look at yourself first."

The Steelers' self-examination and recommitment spurred an eight-game winning streak that vaulted them from playoff long shots to history-making champions: the first No. 6 seed to win a Super Bowl and only the second team to win its first three playoff games on the road, beginning with a 31–17 wild-card triumph over the Bengals. In its stunning divisional-round upset of the top-seeded Indianapolis Colts and its AFC Championship Game drubbing of the second-seeded Denver Broncos, Pittsburgh played at a scarily high level, with big names like Roethlisberger, Polamalu and Porter in starring roles.

Yet Super Sunday belonged to the unheralded Steelers, such lesser lights as second-year halfback Willie Parker, whose 75-yard burst on the second snap of the second half, helped by Pro Bowl left guard Alan Faneca's perfect block on linebacker Leroy Hill, gave Pittsburgh a 14–3 lead. The defensive standouts included Haggans, nosetackle Casey Hampton and cornerback Deshea Townsend, each of whom sacked Seahawks quarterback Matt Hasselbeck, and cornerback Ike Taylor, who atoned for several early lapses in coverage by snagging an interception at the Steelers' five-yard line with 10:46 remaining and his team clinging to a 14–10 advantage.

Four plays after that, the Steelers' biggest pass since Terry Bradshaw hit John Stallworth in Super Bowl XIV was thrown not by Roethlisberger (9 of 21, 123 yards, two interceptions) but by wideout Antwaan Randle El, a former standout quarterback at Indiana whose 43-yard strike to Ward provided the game's signature moment. Credit another perfectly timed call by red-hot offensive coordinator Ken Whisenhunt, who two plays earlier had set up the trick pass by calling a speed screen to Randle El for a seven-yard gain. Then, on first-and-10 from the Seattle 43, Whisenhunt sent in Zero Strong Z Short Fake Toss 39 X Reverse Pass, which was run out of the same formation as the speed screen. "I was so excited," Randle El said later, "I had to make sure I didn't give it away."

FROM LEFT: BOB ROSATO; JOHN W. MCDONOUGH

After Roethlisberger pitched the ball to Parker on the left side, Randle El swung around from his position wide to the left to take a handoff from Parker, then continued rolling to his right as Ward flashed open between three confused defenders. *Throw it to me now!* Ward thought to himself. *Please, please get it to me.* Without breaking stride, Randle El released what he would later call the "prettiest pass" of his life, a tight spiral that Ward caught on the run just inside the Seattle five-yard line, beyond the pursuit of cornerback Marcus Trufant, and cruised in for the game's final points, with 8:56 remaining.

It was a redemptive moment for Ward, whose earlier mishandling of two Roethlisberger passes had symbolized Pittsburgh's offensive futility. The Steelers went nearly four minutes into the second quarter before finally making a first down, while the Seahawks reached their own 47 or deeper on five of their six first-half possessions. But Seattle

160

Randle El (82), a former college QB, took a reverse handoff and found Ward streaking behind a befuddled Seahawks defense for a 43-yard touchdown to put the Steelers up 11 in the fourth quarter.

came away with only three points before intermission, as a combination of dropped passes and costly penalties—including a questionable offensive pass interference call on wideout Darrell Jackson that nullified his apparent 16-yard touchdown reception with two minutes left in the first quarter—kept Hasselbeck (26 of 49, 273 yards) from capitalizing. Indeed, with a number of borderline or puzzling calls, the referees' performance appeared as flat as that of the teams, and when the Rolling Stones blasted their new song *Rough Justice* during the

band's halftime set, Mick Jagger seemed to be singing to the Seahawks.

Though Roethlisberger had played brilliantly in the first three postseason games, Seattle coach Mike Holmgren based his defensive strategy on the premise that the young passer wouldn't replicate his success. "I'd rather put the ball in his hands," Holmgren said last Thursday while sitting in his temporary office at the team's Dearborn hotel. "I can't believe how poorly Denver played in the secondary in the championship game."

For much of the evening Roethlisberger looked like the discombobulated passer who struggled in last year's AFC Championship Game, during which the top-seeded Steelers were dismantled by the New England Patriots—Cowher's fourth loss in five conference title games, all at home. But Big Ben struck at opportune times against the Seahawks. Midway through the second quarter, on third-and-six from the Pittsburgh 45, Roethlisberger's improvised shovel pass to Ward while scrambling to his right resulted in

> "Hines played well, but for the most part it wasn't the big-name guys offensively and defensively."

CLOCKWISE FROM LEFT: AL TIELEMANS; DAVID BERGMAN; DAMIAN STROHMEYER

a 12-yard gain. Later in the drive, on third-and-28 from the Seattle 40, the quarterback dashed to his left to elude Seahawks defensive end Grant Wistrom, pulled up to avoid crossing the line of scrimmage and threw back to the right to Ward at the three-yard line. Three plays later Roethlisberger's lunging keeper gave the Steelers a 7–3 lead.

His one-word postgame assessment of his overall performance: "Ecch."

Roethlisberger cheered up slightly while riding on the team bus to the victory party. "It's not how you picture your Super Bowl moment," he said, "but with this team it had to be that way. Before every game it's, Who's going to step up big today? Hines played well, but for the most part it wasn't the big-name guys offensively and defensively. That's sort of been the M.O. of this team, why it's such a special team and why we won."

Seattle's offense was ranked tops in the NFL, but tight end Jerramy Stevens (86) and friends were brought low by the Steeler defense.

In a season marred by All-Pro wideout Terrell Owens's getting banished by the Philadelphia Eagles after repeated clashes with teammates and coaches, Ward, who turns 30 next month, merely made plays, punishing as many defenders as he could in the process. On Jan. 30, about 12 hours after the Steelers had arrived in Detroit to begin preparations for the Super Bowl, Ward and a group of teammates accompanied Bettis on a late-night trip to Icon, a downtown club. Clad in a green throwback jersey from Bettis's Notre Dame days, Ward chilled in a darkened corner as the Bus soaked up most of

the attention. Noting the off-season departure of receiver Plaxico Burress, a free agent who signed with the New York Giants, Ward said, "For me this season has been about proving I'm a tough player. Without Plax, some people wondered if I could be as effective. I think I've proven I can be."

Ward, whose mother is Korean and father is African-American, then joked that he had a chance to become the "first Asian Super Bowl MVP." He fulfilled that prophecy by making five catches for 123 yards, including a sublime shoestring grab of a Roethlisberger pass early in the third quarter; by delivering a crushing block on cornerback Andre Dyson during Parker's touchdown burst; and, perhaps most impressively of all, by gaining 18 yards on a second-quarter reverse that ended with him and free safety Marquand Manuel crashing into the Seahawks' bench area. "I wanted to hit him," Ward said later of Manuel, who suffered a pulled left groin on the play and did not return. Later, during a third-quarter timeout, Seahawks rookie middle linebacker Lofa Tatupu sauntered up to Ward and said, "I normally don't respect receivers, but I respect you."

The scary thing was that Ward, during practice two days before the game, had sprained a joint in his left shoulder. "It happened when I caught a pass and hit the ground," Ward recounted as he strolled through the cavernous ballroom that housed the Steelers' victory party. "So I decided to take a painkilling shot. Normally I wouldn't do that type of thing, but I wasn't going to miss this game. I still can't lift my arm very high because it's so sore. But you know what? That's really the best kind of pain."

Clad in what he called a "Cab Calloway–style" pin-striped suit, Ward signed autographs and posed for photos. And he got that hug from a country-music icon who might as well have been acting on behalf of the city of Pittsburgh. "This game did a lot for a lot of people," Ward said, his smile as wide as the Monongahela River. "It was big for coach Cowher because people said he couldn't win the big game. It was big for Jerome because it was the last game of his career. It was big for Ben Roethlisberger because people didn't know if a quarterback that young could win this game. And it was big for somebody like me because I was covering kicks when I first came into the league. I look back on those days now, and I feel like I've come a long way."

In two months' time the Steelers came further than anyone could have imagined—all 53 of them, individually and as a team.　　　　✦

Porter (above) rejoiced in the win, as did Cowher, who after 14 seasons in Pittsburgh was able to raise the Lombardi Trophy.

SUPER BOWL

XLIII

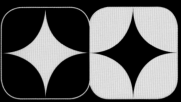

STEELERS 27 ✦ CARDINALS 23

FEBRUARY 1, 2009   RAYMOND JAMES STADIUM, TAMPA

A long, tense replay was needed to confirm that both Holmes's feet were down and in bounds on his game-winning six-yard catch.

JOHN BIEVER

EXCERPTED FROM SPORTS ILLUSTRATED / FEBRUARY 9, 2009

Going For Six the Hard Way

BY **DAMON HACK**

The Steelers needed two of the most extraordinary plays in NFL history to defeat the Cardinals 27–23, winning their sixth title and staking their claim as the greatest team of the Super Bowl era

Polamalu (left) and Taylor (right) clamped down on Fitzgerald, but he burst out late and finished with seven catches for 127 yards and two touchdowns.

BY MIDNIGHT HALF THE TEAM WAS dressed in white Pittsburgh Steelers bathrobes, their fingerprints mucking up a sixth Vince Lombardi Trophy, their cigars burning smoky and sweet. After one of the greatest Super Bowls ever played, wide receiver Santonio Holmes wiped tears from his eyes, owner Dan Rooney pulled on a championship baseball cap and linebacker James Harrison asked if he could fall asleep right there on the locker room floor. Among the quietest in the group was the quarterback, Ben Roethlisberger, who slipped out of the room alone, his robe covering his civilian clothes, the ball with which he knelt to close out Pittsburgh's heart-stopping 27–23 victory over the Arizona Cardinals in Super Bowl XLIII cradled in his left arm.

Three years ago Roethlisberger barely felt a part of the Steelers' fifth Super Bowl title, his play had been so erratic in the victory over the Seattle Seahawks. The football world knew: Pittsburgh had won Super Bowl XL in spite of him. So what does a quarterback think about when he's back in the NFL's showcase game, when his opposite, Kurt Warner, has just found Larry Fitzgerald for a 64-yard touchdown, when his devoted fan base is aching and the clock is ticking down? "Do or die," said Roethlisberger, waiting by the team buses in the Tampa night, recounting his thoughts in the huddle before the Steelers' game-winning drive. "I've said it all along: I want the ball in my hands."

If Harrison's 100-yard interception return can lay claim to being the most remarkable defensive play in 43 Super Bowls, this game will be remembered as well for Roethlisberger's arm, Holmes's tiptoes and the crowning of Pittsburgh as the NFL's marquee franchise of the Super Bowl era.

It will also be recalled as the night Roethlisberger ascended to the cusp of greatness by winning his second Super Bowl at age 26. Trailing 23–20 after the Warner-to-Fitzgerald hookup late in the fourth quarter, Roethlisberger walked onto the field and into the pivotal moment of his career.

Leadership has not always been Roethlisberger's strength, despite his success as the Steelers' starter. As a rookie in 2004 he joined a team stacked with veterans—Hines Ward, Jerome Bettis, Alan Faneca—and had trouble asserting an authoritative voice. While he overcame the deficits in his game with an improvisational flair, a motorcycle accident in June '06 altered his life's trajectory.

Riding his Suzuki Hayabusa through downtown Pittsburgh without a helmet, he collided with a Chrysler New Yorker, sustaining several serious injuries, including broken bones in his face that required two-inch titanium plates and screws to repair. The accident lent him a new perspective. Now, he says, "it's a trophy to be alive every day."

Three years after his poor performance in Detroit in Super Bowl XL, Roethlisberger was a confident and commanding presence, completing 21 of 30 passes and inspiring his teammates in the huddle.

JOHN BIEVER

JOHN BIEVER (3)

Says Ward, "When he steps into the huddle, it's his team. When he steps into the huddle, all eyes are on him."

Roethlisberger's style is not always pretty, which may be why he has developed a kinship with his much-maligned offensive line. Though he was sacked 46 times in the regular season, second-most in the league, Roethlisberger time and again has gone out of his way to defend the men in front of him. Super Bowl week was no different. On the Tuesday before the game he treated his blockers to dinner at P.F. Chang's in Tampa's trendy Westshore Plaza, where the group occupied four tables in the middle of the bustling restaurant. Over fried rice and crispy honey chicken, the men spoke about the past and the future. "We talked about how far we had come and where we wanted to end up," said second-year right guard Darnell Stapleton. Added third-year right tackle Willie Colon, "We said we can't go back to Pittsburgh without [the trophy]."

When the group huddled with 2:30 remaining in the fourth quarter, Colon said, they looked at one another and smiled. What they had talked about at dinner was now in their control. Roethlisberger spoke up: "It's now or never."

Holmes also felt the weight of the moment. "Ben," he told his quarterback, "I want the ball in my hands no matter what."

His quarterback obliged. From the Pittsburgh 12-yard line, Roethlisberger lined up in the shotgun and masterfully directed his charges downfield, pump-faking and shifting in the pocket as his linemen held their ground. On first-and-20 he hit Holmes for 14 yards. On third-and-six he found Holmes for 13 more. Three plays later from the Cardinals' 46, Roethlisberger spotted Holmes open about 10 yards downfield. The third-year wideout took the short pass, spun to his left and raced to the Arizona six.

First-and-goal, 48 seconds to play. Roethlisberger dropped back and whistled a pass to the back of the end zone that slipped through the hands of the leaping Holmes.

On the next play, with the Steelers' line keeping the Cardinals' rush at bay, Roethlisberger had time to run through his progression. His first read, running back Willie Parker, was covered in the flat. His second option, receiver Nate Washington, also had too many red jerseys around him. So Roethlisberger looked to his third option, Holmes, and saw him racing to the right corner of the end zone. Three defenders were in front of the receiver, but Roethlisberger fired the ball anyway, high and outside. Holmes snagged it with his fingertips and touched the grass with both sets of outstretched toes. His fourth catch of the drive and ninth

Harrison's 100-yard runback was all the more dramatic because it came as time expired in the first half and would have led to no Pittsburgh points if Fitzgerald had stopped him a foot shorter.

reception of the night was the game-winner—and good enough to make Holmes the Super Bowl MVP.

"[Roethlisberger] put it where only Tone could have caught it," said Pittsburgh offensive coordinator Bruce Arians on the field after the game. He then drew some parallels to Steelers past. "Tone is Swann, Hines is Stallworth—and don't forget, we got a Bradshaw too. Ben showed that tonight."

I f Holmes, Ward and Roethlisberger recall Lynn Swann, John Stallworth and Terry Bradshaw from the four-time champs of the '70s, coach Mike Tomlin is the ideal successor to Chuck Noll and Bill Cowher. In the swirling story lines of Super Bowl week—among them his own showdown with Cardinals coach Ken Whisenhunt and assistant Russ Grimm, two former Steelers staffers who had been in contention for the Pittsburgh job in 2007—Tomlin kept his players both focused and loose. It was the continuation of his imprint on the Steelers brand.

To understand how he became, at 36, the youngest coach to win a Super Bowl, draw a direct line to Pittsburgh's wild-card loss at home to Jacksonville one year ago. That the Steelers had cracked at Heinz Field in the postseason, in familiar wintry conditions, stung badly. Some veterans felt Tomlin's coaching style that first year—long practices, banging in pads—had burned out his players before the Jaguars game. "Last year against Jacksonville," said Colon, "we kind of crawled into that game."

Said 12th-year linebacker James Farrior, "We all understand that when you're coming in as a new coach, you have to do it your way. We didn't like it sometimes, and it was tough sometimes, but it was something we had to deal with. This year [he's known] when to push our buttons and when to lay off. When he gives us breaks, we all feel like we have to uphold the responsibility and not be the guy who goes out and gets in trouble. He's a hard-nosed coach, but he gives us that [leeway] to go out and do the things we love to do, and he doesn't really put restrictions on us. We love him for that."

Ward was one of several veterans whom Tomlin excused from Wednesday practices during the season. That was a nod to the trust that developed between the young coach and his players. Still, Tomlin does not apologize for his firm hand. "I'm committed to winning," he said last

> " [Tomlin] talked about embracing the moment and honoring the legacies of players who came before. "

week. "I'm committed to playing a brand of football that I believe in. It's a physical game. You win by attrition. You impose your will on your opponent. That's what I want our [game] tape to look like."

Not that Tomlin won't occasionally sprinkle in some humor. On the Friday before the Steelers arrived in Tampa, Harrison and cornerback Bryant McFadden were goofing off in the locker room, standing nose-to-nose in a stare-down as their teammates cheered them on. Soon Tomlin joined the group, hooting and hollering as boisterously as his players.

Once the Steelers arrived in Tampa, they seemed at ease both on the practice field and in the crush of media. On Wednesday, Roethlisberger brought a video camera to Harrison's podium and pointed it at the NFL's Defensive Player of the Year.

"Uh, Mr. Harrison, do you like to beat up cameramen?" the quarterback asked.

"Only if it's Ben Roethlisberger," Harrison replied.

Holmes's tiptoe catch in the back corner of the end zone with 35 seconds left sealed the win and his Super Bowl MVP award.

While some coaches shield their players as much as possible from distractions during the buildup to the Super Bowl, Tomlin invited 250 of the Steelers' friends and relatives to watch Pittsburgh's 38-minute walkthrough on the day before the game. Among the attendees was the Reverend Jesse Jackson, who also found his way into the team's postgame celebration.

"He has [the players'] mothers, fathers, grandparents, uncles and aunts to build a community," Jackson said of Tomlin. "At his age, he has a rapport with his players that is unusual. Because he's so young, his genius is covered up."

But its effects are evident—especially on defense, where Tomlin's Steelers create the same mayhem as always. He and coordinator Dick LeBeau ask for versatility from their players, and the pass-rushing Harrison epitomizes that. A special-teamer on the Super Bowl XL team, Harrison, 30, has emerged as one of the NFL's hardest defenders to scheme against. All night he disrupted Arizona's plans, forcing left tackle Mike Gandy into three holding penalties and, with fellow linebackers Farrior, Larry Foote and LaMarr Woodley, putting near-constant pressure on Warner.

But the league's No. 1 defense still had problems against the Cardinals, thanks to their array of elusive receivers and backs, and to the poise of their 37-year-old quarterback. All week Warner had been the vision of calm, carrying a note from his 17-year-old daughter, Jesse, in the front sleeve of his playbook: "Dad, I just wanted to let you know how proud I am of you. I'm so thankful and honored to be your daughter. I'll be praying for you. You deserve everything you want and probably more. I love you so much. Go Cards! Love, Jesse."

Warner carried those thoughts onto the field, coolly connecting with second and third options when the Steelers stacked their coverage against Fitzgerald. For most of the first half Pittsburgh flip-flopped cornerback Ike Taylor and safety Troy Polamalu, giving Fitzgerald several looks at the line of scrimmage. Warner adjusted, riding Anquan Boldin and Steve Breaston in the opening quarters and cutting Pittsburgh's lead to 10–7 on a one-yard pass to Ben Patrick.

Then came a critical turning point. After Roethlisberger was intercepted on a pass deflection, Warner moved the Cardinals into position to score again in the waning moments of the first half. With Arizona on

Holmes celebrated by imitating LeBron James's chalk toss, while Farrior and Foote (above) enjoyed Rooney-esque cigars.

the Pittsburgh one and 18 seconds remaining, Harrison dropped into coverage rather than coming on the rush and stepped right into the path of Warner's pass to Boldin. Taking off down the right sideline, he dodged Warner, Fitzgerald, Breaston, Gandy, tight end Leonard Pope, guard Reggie Wells and the churning legs of his own teammates. When Fitzgerald and Breaston finally caught Harrison short of the goal line, the linebacker did a somersault over Fitzgerald, landing on his head to score the touchdown. For several long moments Harrison lay on his back, palms up, toes pointing skyward. Tomlin headed for the end zone, where he helped Harrison to his feet and walked him off the field, an arm draped over the linebacker's shoulder. "It was tiring," Harrison said of his historic run, "but it was all worth it."

At halftime, Tomlin gathered his players. He talked about embracing the moment and honoring the legacy of the players who'd come before, players like Swann and Bettis, both of whom were on the field before kickoff. There were reminders of Steelers football everywhere in Tampa. Tens of thousands of towel-waving, Black-and-Gold-clad fans had descended upon the area, escaping a harsh winter and a harsh economy for a few days at least. And while Super Bowl week might have been subdued, the football on the field was both familiar and magical.

Harrison's mad dash recalled Franco Harris's Immaculate Reception. Holmes and Ward channeled the dramatics of Swann and Stallworth. Tomlin's jaw was as firm-set as Cowher's. Roethlisberger pulled halfway to Bradshaw's four rings with a mettle that, like Bradshaw's, might not be truly appreciated until after he's gone.

As for trophy number 6, which set Pittsburgh apart from five-time winners Dallas and San Francisco, it was still being manhandled far beyond midnight.

"You all passed the sticky Lombardi around? I ain't even touched it!" Tomlin yelled before heading to the buses.

Soon the Lombardi Trophy would be making its way to western Pennsylvania, where it would be driven across town, over the Hot Metal Bridge, down South Water Street and dropped off at the third building on the right.

It is there that the coach's office sits close to a trophy case that is about to grow larger. Where a dynasty born in a long-ago winter is young again. ✦

STAR ATTRACTIONS

WHAT JINX? DESPITE MORE THAN 40 SI COVER APPEARANCES (36 SHOWN HERE), THE STEELERS HAVE SOMEHOW MANAGED TO DO ALL RIGHT FOR THEMSELVES

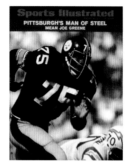

OCTOBER 11, 1971

JULY 29, 1974

SEPTEMBER 23, 1974

JANUARY 6, 1975

JANUARY 20, 1975

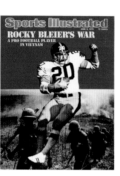

JUNE 9, 1975

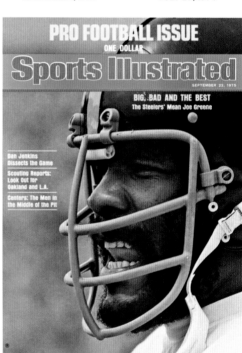

SEPTEMBER 22, 1975

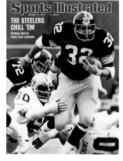

JANUARY 12, 1976

JANUARY 26, 1976

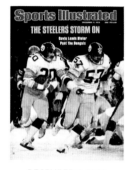

DECEMBER 6, 1976

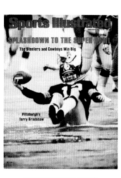

JANUARY 15, 1979

JANUARY 29, 1979

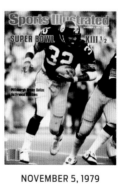

NOVEMBER 5, 1979

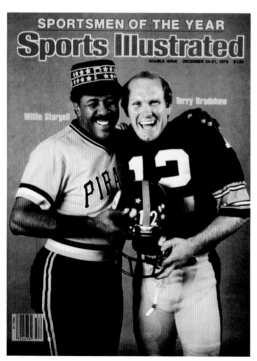

DECEMBER 24, 1979

JANUARY 14, 1980

JANUARY 28, 1980

NOVEMBER 10, 1980

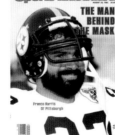

AUGUST 23, 1982

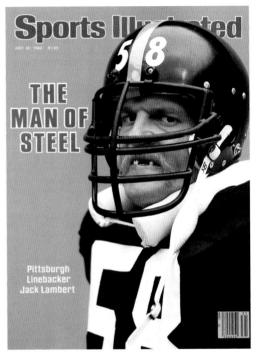

THE MAN OF STEEL

Pittsburgh
Linebacker
Jack Lambert

JULY 30, 1984

JANUARY 7, 1985

DECEMBER 5, 1994

NOVEMBER 24, 1997

DECEMBER 10, 2001

NOVEMBER 15, 2004

NOVEMBER 14, 2005

JANUARY 16, 2006

JANUARY 23, 2006

JANUARY 30, 2006

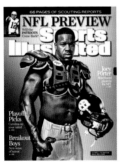

FEBRUARY 13, 2006

SEPTEMBER 4, 2006

DECEMBER 22, 2008

JANUARY 7, 2012

JANUARY 26, 2009

FEBRUARY 9, 2009

JANUARY 31, 2011

SEPTEMBER 5, 2011

T HIS BOOK WOULD NOT HAVE BEEN possible without the efforts of the writers, editors and photographers who have covered the Steelers for SPORTS ILLUSTRATED for nearly six decades. Special thanks for their generous help also goes to Geoff Michaud, Dan Larkin, Bob Thompson and the entire SI imaging group; Jay Soysal, Dwayne Bernard and Trevor Lazarus of the SI art department; and Steve Finc, George Washington, Karen Carpenter, Prem Kalliat, Joe Felice, George Amores and Will Welt of the SI photo and picture syndication departments. Our gratitude goes as well to Burt Lauten and Karl Roser of the Pittsburgh Steelers, to Saleem Choudhry at the Pro Football Hall of Fame and to Time Inc. Sports Group editor Terry McDonell.

Grateful acknowledgment is also made to the following for permission to reprint copyrighted material:

He Does What He Wants Out There Copyright © 1975 by Roy Blount Jr. *True Tales of the Terrible Towel* Copyright © 1979 by Myron Cope. Used by permission of the author's family

WALTER IOOSS JR.

Mean Joe Greene's 1981 helmet